PAUL AND JAMES

STUDIES IN BIBLICAL THEOLOGY · 46

PAUL AND JAMES

WALTER SCHMITHALS

WIPF & STOCK · Eugene, Oregon

Wipf and Stock Publishers
199 W 8th Ave, Suite 3
Eugene, OR 97401

Paul and James
By Schmithals, Walther
Copyright©1965 SCM Press
ISBN 13: 978-1-60899-028-3
Publication date 9/24/2009
Previously published by SCM Press, 1965

Copyright © SCM Press 1965
First English edition 1965 by SCM Press
This Edition published by arrangement with SCM-Canterbury Press

IN MEMORIAM
Professor Dr Theol. Hans Günter Grünweller
nat. 1926   ob. 1961

CONTENTS

	Preface to the English Edition	9
	Abbreviations	11
	Introductory: Paul and James	13
I	Stephen	16
II	The 'Apostolic Council'	38
III	The Unfortunate Incident in Antioch	63
IV	The Collection of the Contributions	79
V	Paul's Last Visit to Jerusalem	85
VI	The 'Apostolic Decree'	97
VII	Judaizers?	103
	Bibliography	119
	Index of Authors	123
	Index of New Testament Passages Discussed	125

PREFACE TO THE ENGLISH EDITION

THIS small book represents the temporary conclusion of a series of studies dealing with the relationships between the parties in the primitive Christian Church. A list of these studies which began with an investigation of Gnosticism in Corinth will be found in the Bibliography. *Die Gnosis in Korinth* is about to appear in a revised edition; the shorter studies have been re-examined, corrected and supplemented, an essay on 'Die historische Situation der Thessalonicherbriefe' has been added, and all will be published together in one volume, *Paulus und die Gnostiker* (1965).

In all these studies we have been concerned with the problem of the identity of the opponents with whom Paul is grappling in his mission area. Contrary to the prevailing opinion today, it emerges from these studies that F. C. Baur was right in considering that all the genuine Pauline letters showed a uniform hostile attitude. At the same time it is nevertheless clear that these opponents are not Judaizers, but Jews or Jewish Christians with a pronounced Gnostic trend who stood in no kind of relationship to the Jewish Christians in Palestine.

Consequently Paul's relation to the primitive church in Jerusalem must be examined afresh. This has been done in the study presented here, which appeared in Germany in 1963. Its English edition has been looked through, slightly amended and extended. Even if it should be seen and read in close association with the earlier studies mentioned above, yet it has been worked out without depending on them; the exegesis in it should therefore also be judged independently of them.

As the dedication shows, this book is at the same time intended to be a modest memorial to a friendship broken off prematurely.

WALTER SCHMITHALS

ABBREVIATIONS

ARW	*Archiv für Religionswissenschaft*, Leipzig
BZ	*Biblische Zeitschrift*, Freiburg
BZNW	Beihefte zur *ZNW*
ET	English translation
EvTh	*Evangelische Theologie*, Munich
ExpT	*Expository Times*, Edinburgh
FRLANT	Forschungen zur Religion und Literatur des Alten und Neuen Testaments, Göttingen
HNT	Handbuch zum Neuen Testament, Tübingen
Meyer	Kritisch-exegetischer Kommentar über das Neue Testament, begründet von H. A. W. Meyer, Göttingen
NGG	*Nachrichten von der Gesellschaft der Wissenschaften zu Göttingen*
NTD	Das Neue Testament Deutsch, Göttingen
NTS	*New Testament Studies*, Cambridge
PG	Migne, Patrologia Graeca, Paris
RAC	*Reallexikon für Antike und Christentum*, Stuttgart, 1941ff.
RGG	*Die Religion in Geschichte und Gegenwart*³, Tübingen, 1957ff.
SBA	*Sitzungsberichte der . . . Akademie der Wissenschaften zu Berlin*
SBT	Studies in Biblical Theology, London
THKNT	Theologischer Handkommentar zum Neuen Testament, Berlin
TLZ	*Theologische Literaturzeitung*, Leipzig
TR	*Theologische Rundschau*, Tübingen

Abbreviations

TWNT	*Theologisches Wörterbuch zum Neuen Testament*, ed. G. Kittel, Stuttgart, 1932ff.
TZ	*Theologische Zeitschrift*, Basel
VF	*Verkündigung und Forschung*, Munich
WMANT	*Wissenschaftliche Monographien zum Alten und Neuen Testament*, Neukirchen
ZKG	*Zeitschrift für Kirchengeschichte*, Stuttgart
ZNW	*Zeitschrift für die neutestamentliche Wissenschaft*, Berlin
ZTK	*Zeitschrift für Theologie und Kirche*, Tübingen

The **bold** figures at the head of each page are those of the pages of the German edition.

Introductory:

PAUL AND JAMES

THE historical conclusions of the exegetical labours of F. C. Baur are still today an important influence when scholars examine the relation of Paul to James, that is to say, the relation of the Hellenistic churches founded by Paul to the primitive Jewish-Christian church in Jerusalem.[1] According to F. C. Baur it was the Judaizers from Jerusalem who must be held responsible for the violent controversies in the Pauline mission area of which we learn in the Pauline letters. The verdict of 'false apostles', 'servants of Satan' (II Cor. 11.13ff.), is aimed directly at the original apostles in Jerusalem. Thereby an unequivocal verdict is passed on the relationship of Paul to James.

It has long been recognized that this verdict of the Tübingen school cannot be maintained. It is true that there exists today less unanimity than ever concerning the nature and backgrounds of the anti-Pauline activities in Galatia and Corinth, Philippi and Thessalonica; but hardly anyone who reads the Pauline letters still dares to see in the Jerusalem church and its pillars, Peter and James, the opponents of Paul. Whoever takes the usual view, when dealing with the agitation, whether great or small, of the Judaizers against Paul, generally attributes the responsibility for it to a separate extremist movement amongst the Palestinian Jewish Christians. If those who carry on a mission in opposition to the Pauline churches are regarded as Hellenistic or Gnostic Jewish Christians, or even as Judaizing Gentile Christians, then for that reason alone any special connexion between these opponents of Paul and the original church in Jerusalem must be disputed. But in that case scholars are faced anew with the problem of the nature of Paul's relation to James, and a fresh examination of it is required.

Of course, work on this task has always been going on. Numerous articles and the relevant sections in the commentaries deal with the pertinent passages, especially in the Pauline *corpus* and the

[1] This is the meaning given to 'Paul' and 'James' in what follows.

Acts of the Apostles, and with the problems raised by these passages. Yet it seems to me to be the particular merit of J. Munck in his book, *Paul and the Salvation of Mankind*, to have raised the question of Paul's relation to James in a comprehensive study, and thereby to have drawn attention to the fact that a complete solution to a problem which the Tübingen school appeared to have settled is still awaited.[2] What Munck himself offers as a solution can indeed hardly be considered as such. He supposes that Paul and James, Gentile Christians and Jewish Christians, always lived and taught in complete harmony. This need not be considered impossible *a priori*, but the often positively fantastic reasoning with which Munck supports his thesis[3] is hardly likely to meet with much agreement.

However, it is, in fact, by no means easy to answer the question we have posed. The Tübingen school had extensive grounds for their opinion in the numerous statements made by Paul in his letters when disputing with his opponents. These grounds have now been abandoned and there remain in particular those occasional remarks in which Paul gives explicit information about his relations with Jerusalem, and the statements in the Acts which must be used only with the utmost circumspection. There are no other sources at our disposal for describing the relation of Paul to James; for today with good reason no one dares to join the Tübingen school in drawing conclusions from later writings, such as the Clementine literature and the supposedly Jewish-Christian apocryphal gospels, as to the relations within the Christian churches before the Jewish revolt. It must also be admitted that the letters of James and Peter, the Revelation and other writings merit no serious attention for providing answers to our problem.

Paul's relationship to the church in Jerusalem is indeed only one special case—although a significant one—of the whole relationship of Jewish to Gentile Christianity. Hence it would be a great help if we had precise information about the whole of this relationship. But this we do not possess, as everyone knows who is acquainted with the history of early Christianity. It is generally recognized today that the above-named and other post-apostolic

---

[2] Pp. 69–86; these pages are the best part of Munck's book and are—on the whole—well worth reading.

[3] For a critique of Munck's book see R. Bultmann's review in *TLZ* 84, 1959, cols. 481–6.

writings do not allow of any kind of reliable inferences regarding any trends in Jewish Christianity before the year 70. It is Paul's particular relations with Jerusalem which form the principal source of our knowledge of those existing in the first century between Gentile and Jewish Christianity as a whole, and not the other way round.

However, one weighty report from the early period which does not deal with the special relation of Paul to James has been handed down to us in the account in the Acts about the martyrdom of Stephen and the events which led up to it, namely, Acts 6.1–8.3. It is true that we do not have to do here with anything like a reliable historical account. Yet we must dare to make the venture and to let this passage introduce us to the problems of the relationship between Jewish and Gentile Christianity as a whole, of which the special case of Paul and James will then monopolize our attention.

I

STEPHEN

1. THE scene described in Acts 6.1–7 provides us with evidence for a division in the original Jerusalem church. Up till then Luke had laid stress on the unity of the church there, e.g. 1.14; 2.1, 46; 4.32; 5.12 *et passim*. Moreover, he proceeds to make the apostles put an end promptly to the incipient quarrels. This fact shows at once that Luke cannot simply have invented the scene in Acts 6.1–7 which conflicts with his special purpose,[1] as H. G. Schoeps supposes.[1a]

The church is divided into Ἑβραῖοι and Ἑλληνισταί. We are not told the difference between them. The term Ἑλληνιστής is attested for the first time in Acts. Usually, as already in Chrysostom,[2] these two terms are thought to show the distinction between Hebrew- and Greek-speaking Jews or Jewish Christians.[3] That might also be Luke's opinion. Yet Luke when using them may not necessarily have hit upon the original meaning, and we shall soon see that the real contrast between the 'Hebrews' and the 'Hellenists' did not consist in differences of language. H. J. Cadbury[4] has already strongly challenged that explanation; he states that the designation Ἑβραῖοι is in universal use for the Jews as a whole, even for Greek-speaking Jews.[5] Hence according to Cadbury we must reckon with the possibility that the division in the Jerusalem church, to which Acts 6.1–7 testifies, was between

---

[1] Cf. E. Haenchen, pp. 222f. 219f.; M. Simon, *St Stephen and the Hellenists*, p. 4.
[1a] *Theologie und Geschichte des Judenchristentums*, pp. 439ff.; *Urgemeinde, Judenchristentum, Gnosis*, pp. 5f., 13.
[2] *Hom.* 14 on Acts 6.1 (PG 60, col. 113).
[3] C. F. D. Moule, 'Once More, Who were the Hellenists?' *ExpT* 70, 1959, pp. 100ff., makes a more precise distinction between the Hellenists who were Jews knowing *only* the Greek language and the Hebrews who may possibly have spoken Greek as well, but in any case spoke a Semitic language. W. G. Kümmel agrees with this in *RGG* VI³, col. 1189f.
[4] 'The Hellenists', in *The Beginnings of Christianity* V (1933), pp. 59–74. Cf. H. Windisch in *TWNT* II, p. 508f.; M. Simon, pp. 9ff.
[5] W. Bauer, *Rechtgläubigkeit*, p. 56; cf. K. G. Kuhn and W. Gutbrod in *TWNT* III, 366–70, 374ff., 391–4.

Jewish Christians and Gentile Christians. In that case Ἑλληνισταί =Ἕλληνες, which in most manuscripts is attested for the first time in Acts 11.20.[6] We cannot come to a definite decision on this question here.[7] We shall return to it.

That the dissatisfaction over the provision for the widows can never have been the cause of the division in the church as recorded by Luke has been proved so convincingly by the brilliant exegesis of Haenchen,[8] following others, that we can regard this question as settled. If this dispute did, in fact, ever take place, it was only a concrete expression of latent tensions.[9]

The seven deacons, obviously all Hellenists,[10] have nothing special to do with the relief of the poor, as the rest of Luke's account itself enables us to realize. They were evangelists: 6.8ff.; 8.5ff.; 21.8.[11] Besides, it would also be extremely strange if the office of deacon in the whole Jerusalem church had been entrusted to Hellenists alone, as Luke's account presupposes. We must consider the seven to be the leaders of the Hellenistic section of the church; this is the universal assumption of scholars today.[12] Thus this Hellenistic section of the community separated itself from the 'original church'.

---

[6] Additional references in *TWNT* II, 509, lines 5ff. The same opinion as that of Cadbury was already expressed by G. P. Wetter, *ARW* 21, 1922, especially on pp. 410ff. He was supported by W. Grundmann in *ZNW* 38, 1939, pp. 54ff.

[7] We may also allude to B. Reicke's compromise hypothesis, which sees in the Hellenists principally former proselytes (*Glaube und Leben der Urgemeinde*, pp. 116f.).

[8] Pp. 223ff./218ff.

[9] Cf. on this now Haenchen, 13th ed., pp. 221f.

[10] They all bear Greek names. Were they all proselytes like Nicolaus? In that case special attention is called to him not simply because he was a proselyte but because he came from Antioch. (Thus B. Reicke, p. 117; cf. W. Grundmann, p. 57.) Or is Nicolaus called a proselyte because the others were Jews by birth? (Thus Haenchen, pp. 220/217, and most other commentators.) Or is the proselyte Nicolaus distinguished from the other Hellenists because he was the only one who was circumcised, whilst all the others were uncircumcised Gentile Christians? (Cf. Wetter, p.412.) Unfortunately this question, too, remains open here.

[11] Haenchen, pp. 225/219; H. Lietzmann, *The Beginnings of the Christian Church*, ET, 3rd ed., 1953, pp. 70f.; R. Bultmann, *Theology* I, p. 56; M. Simon, *Stephen*, pp. 6f.; C. T. Craig, *The Beginnings of Christianity*, 1943, p. 147; J. Weiss, *Die Apostelgeschichte*, pp. 10f.; W. Schrage, 'Ekklesia und Synagoge', *ZTK* 60, 1963, p. 197.

[12] Recently M. Simon, pp. 6ff. It is not *a priori* impossible that the Hellenists first organized themselves as a group of their own under the leadership of the 'seven' because of the dispute concerning the provision for the widows, as Haenchen assumes, p. 226. If Cadbury were correct and they were, in fact, Gentile Christians, they must no doubt have been organized independently from the beginning. That could almost certainly be taken for granted if the Hellenists had command of only Greek, or if their theological attitude was materially different from that of the 'Hebrews'.

But now questions arise.

How could such a special group come into being in Jerusalem? Haenchen[13] has good reason to write: 'What causes astonishment is that the Hellenists ventured to strike out, that they emerged from this magnetic field.' What presuppositions account for this development?

Furthermore: Wherein lay the real differences between 'Hebrews' and 'Hellenists', of which no word is said, at any rate in Acts 6.1–7?

And finally: Why does Luke pass these differences over in silence? Why does he also not tell us anything about the rise of the Hellenists? Because he did not know anything about it? At any rate he knows more about it than appears in Acts 6.1–7. For this is evident from the continuation of his account concerning Stephen.

2. There is no doubt that for his account of Stephen's martyrdom which now follows Luke is making use of an existing tradition. This is clear from the fact that the mention of the Hellenistic Jews who dispute with Stephen is not accounted for by what has already been described in the Acts, for after all Stephen, too, was very far from being introduced by Luke as a Hellenist in Acts 6.1–7.[14] Besides, the description of Stephen as a powerful preacher is the direct opposite of the Lucan design in 6.1–7, which represents him as in charge of the almsgiving, whilst preaching is said to be the business of the apostles.

Stephen's great speech does not belong to this tradition, any more, in fact, than the whole proceedings before the council, which have been interpolated into the traditional account.[15] Moreover, the references in the speech to the accusations brought against Stephen according to Acts 6.11 are exceedingly scarce.[16]

---

[13] 10th ed., p. 227; cf. 13th ed., p. 222.
[14] See again Haenchen, pp. 230f./220.
[15] H. H. Wendt, *Apostelgeschichte*, p. 134 n. 2; Haenchen, pp. 232/226; H. Thyen, *Der Stil der Jüdisch-Hellenistischen Homilie* (FRLANT 65), 1955, pp. 19f.; M. Dibelius, *Acts*, pp. 167–70.
[16] W. Foerster, 'Stephanus und die Urgemeinde', in *Dienst unter dem Wort*, pp. 9–30, actually makes this speech the basis of his thesis; according to this the difference between Hebrews and Hellenists consisted in the view held only by the latter that a fresh Jewish exile preceded by the destruction of the Temple was to be expected. This explanation will hardly win approval. Apart from all the other difficulties of this hypothesis, such an expectation on the part of a community waiting for the parousia can hardly be imagined.

In connexion with Stephen's martyrdom 'a great persecution arose against the church in Jerusalem' (Acts 8.1). Since Luke always presented Stephen to his readers as a representative of the whole Jerusalem church, the persecution must in consequence strike the church as a whole. That is what Luke also supposes in 8.1: 'they were all scattered'. Now we know that Stephen by no means represented all the Jerusalem Christians, but only the Hellenist section of them. We know in addition that the relationship of this section to the 'Hebrews' was not free from tension. So we must allow for the possibility that the persecution only struck the Hellenists. That this was, in fact, the case is shown by Luke himself when he remarks that all were scattered πλὴν τῶν ἀποστόλων (8.1). Now it is, of course, quite unthinkable that the whole church was scattered, and that their leaders could remain unmolested in Jerusalem. The opposite might be credible. Thus πλὴν τῶν ἀποστόλων is a Lucan interpretation.[17]

Is this remark only intended to secure the continuity, so exceedingly important to Luke theologically, of the church, or rather of the apostolic authority in Jerusalem, and was it, in fact, the whole church that was thought to be scattered? This is hardly possible! Neither in the Acts nor in the Pauline letters is there preserved any trace of a tradition from which we might conclude that the original church had been obliged to leave Jerusalem in the early days as a body, and had only been allowed to return again later. So the generally accepted hypothesis is more probable that the phrase πλὴν τῶν ἀποστόλων is intended to minimize the fact, conflicting with Luke's concern, that the persecution fell only upon a section of the church. Since Stephen was the head of this section, those who were persecuted can only have been the Hellenists. The 'Hebrews', not only their leaders, remained unmolested.[18]

3. But if this is the case, then there is all the more reason for the question: What was the nature of that material difference between 'Hebrews' and 'Hellenists', which would explain not only the division in the original church, but also the marked difference in their treatment by the Jews. It is obvious that to point to a difference in the mother tongue of each group gives no help. Haenchen

---

[17] Cf. Simon, *Stephen*, p. 27; F. F. Bruce, *The Acts of the Apostles*, 1956², p. 181, supposes that the apostles had held out at their post from a sense of duty. Similarly G. B. Caird, *The Apostolic Age*, 1958, p. 87.
[18] Haenchen, pp. 256/248; Bultmann, *Theology* I, p. 56.

in his excellent analysis of Stephen's story has dealt with this question, too. He is aware of the fact that 'there was a deep-seated difference—this is proved by the persecution—between the "gospel" of the Hellenists and that of the Hebrews'.[19] More precisely, it follows from the persecution of the Hellenists 'that their "gospel" necessarily contained something which the Jews could not bear and which was lacking in the preaching of the "Hebrews".'[19a] What was this special feature in the Hellenists' preaching?

The pre-Lucan tradition of the story about Stephen gives us a hint when speaking of the headings of the accusation against Stephen. Admittedly we possess this tradition only in Luke's version and Luke is very much concerned to water down the accusations against Stephen.[20] We can see this already in the fact that he attributes them to 'false witnesses' instigated to make this statement (Acts 6.11ff.) and that he refutes the main point of the accusation by his interpolations into Stephen's great speech.[20a] These declare that it was not the Christians but the Jews themselves who rejected Moses and the Law. It is certainly also a Lucan interpretation that these false charges have as their subject-matter blasphemous remarks against Moses and God (6.11). The most likely content of the charge was that Stephen was speaking against the Temple and the Law, which Luke expresses in concrete terms: Jesus will destroy the Temple and change the Mosaic customs. These are words which are the opposite of the attitude of the primitive Church to the Temple and Law as described by Luke up till then.[21] That is, of course, why he makes 'false witnesses' bring them up against Stephen. But that is the very reason why their original form proves them to be part of a pre-Lucan tradition, even though their present formulation is Lucan, as is shown by comparing them with Acts 21.28.[22]

Haenchen agreed with the bulk of scholars in thinking that this was the peculiarity of the Hellenists' preaching and the reason for

---

[19] 10th ed., p. 226; cf. 13th ed., pp. 220f.
[19a] *Loc. cit.*
[20] The motives inspiring this concern are touched upon below; see p. 32 n. 65.
[20a] According to Haenchen, pp. 246ff./240, we owe vv. 35, 37, 39–43, 48–53 to the hand of Luke.
[21] Cf. H. Conzelmann, *The Theology of St Luke*, ET, 1960, pp. 164f.
[22] See below, p. 27.

their persecution,[23] especially as both things have a disparaging reference made to them again (7.48, 53).[24] Klein raised objections to this view of the matter in his review of Haenchen's commentary.[25]

Any Jew might announce the abolition of the Temple at the end of time. It was even not uncommon in Jewry to have only a slight regard for the cult and its sacrifices. Judaism had for long been a religion not of the cult, but of the Law. Already the Old Testament contains plenty of criticism: I Kings 8.27; I Sam. 15.22; Pss. 40.6; 50.8ff.; 51.17; Isa. 1.11ff.; 66.1; Jer. 7.21f.; Hos. 6.6; Micah 6.6–8. The Essenes at the gates of the Holy City persistently disregarded the Temple cult without being molested on that account,[26] not to mention the Galileans and particularly the Samaritans. The Hellenistic Jews had only a very loose relationship to the Temple cult; Justin (*Dial.* 117.2) mentions that Jewish circles in the Diaspora had interpreted Mal. 1.10ff. to mean that God had rejected the sacrificial cult in Jerusalem in favour of the prayers offered by the Jews in the dispersion.[27] The critical attitude towards the Temple shown in Stephen's speech is not, in fact, generally Jewish, but neither is it un-Jewish.[28] After all, Judaism survived the destruction of the Temple without a great convulsion. This question in particular could not open a chasm between 'Hebrews' and 'Hellenists'. Whatever may be the truth of Luke's idea that the original church gathered in the Temple, even he cannot maintain that they took part regularly in the sacrificial worship.[29]

Similarly it was by no means already a crime involving the death sentence to dispute about individual regulations of the Mosaic

[23] 10th ed., p. 226.
[24] *Loc. cit.*
[25] *ZKG* 68, 1957, p. 368.
[26] The reason for this disregard of the Temple cult is indeed said to be that the present cult in Jerusalem defiles the holy place. But it is just the criticism implied by this disregard of the Temple to which Judaism is prepared to consent.
[27] Cf. also *Orac. Sib.* IV 8ff., 24ff., and G. Strecker, *Judenchristentum*, pp. 183f.
[28] R. Bultmann, *Das Evangelium des Johannes*, p. 88 n. 7; G. Friedrich, 'Messianische Hohepriestererwartung in den Synoptikern', *ZTK*, 1956, pp. 289ff. It has therefore been maintained not without good grounds that in the case of Stephen's speech, *including* the passages which criticize the Law, we have to do with a discourse which originated in a Hellenistic synagogue and was used by Luke (H. Thyen, *Der Stil der Jüdisch-Hellenistischen Homilie*, pp. 19f.). Cf. also Simon, *Stephen*, pp. 84ff.; P. Dalbert, *Missionsliteratur*, pp. 65, 115, 136.
[29] Admittedly Matt. 5.23 might contain a hint that the Jerusalem Christians did not withdraw from the sacrificial cult *on principle*.

Law or to ignore them. Even in Palestine Jewry did not consist only of Pharisees, and even these debated about the Law. It is still true to say of the Jesus of the synoptists: 'His critical interpretation of the Law . . . in spite of its radicality likewise stands within the scribal discussion of it.'[30] The 'people of the land' were certainly circumcised and thereby also included in the Jewish national community, but they were by no means strict about keeping the Law. The verdict on this *am haaretz* was certainly: 'This crowd who do not know the Law are accursed' (John 7.49);[31] yet, of course, they were not subjected to the same fate as Stephen. Even priests were often numbered amongst these *am haaretz*.[31a] If a certain laxity in observing or esteeming the Law had brought Stephen to his death, it would have been consistent to depopulate half Palestine. 'Galilee, Galilee, you hate the teaching; you will end up by belonging to the robbers' is a significant rabbinic statement (see in Billerbeck I, p. 157). The fact that strict and lax Jews lived side by side did certainly lead to difficulties, as the comprehensive material in Billerbeck shows; but all the same they did not kill each other.[32] Hellenistic Jewry went farther in some places than the *am haaretz* in freeing itself from the restraints of the Law, without being persecuted on that account.[33] One need only think of Philo, who—in his own way—justified freedom from the Law theologically. How far removed from all the apocalyptic writings[34] are the Temple and the Law as understood by the Pharisees![35]

We certainly cannot go wrong if we assume that the 'Hebrews' in Jerusalem, too, cannot have been *strict* as regards the Law,

[30] R. Bultmann, *Theology* I, pp. 34f.; cf. A. v. Harnack, *The Mission and Expansion of Christianity*, ET 1908, p. 51.
[31] See on this R. Bultmann, *Das Evangelium des Johannes*, pp. 234f.; Billerbeck II, pp. 494-519; R. Meyer, 'Der Am haares', *Judaica* 3, 1947, pp. 169-99.
[31a] Billerbeck II, p. 495.
[32] On this question recently cf. E. Käsemann, 'Zum Thema der urchristlichen Apokalyptik', *ZTK* 59, 1962, pp. 266f.; P. Winter, *On the Trial of Jesus*, Berlin, 1961, pp. 129ff.
[33] See p. 29 n. 56.
[34] Cf. on this the excellent study of D. Rössler, *Gesetz und Geschichte* (WMANT 3), 1960.
[35] The Jewry of the New Testament period was no unity and before the destruction of the Temple there was no Jewish orthodoxy. At that time, if my view is correct, the bloody altercations within Judaism always had a mainly *political* aspect, not a theological one, as is illustrated for us here by the question of the Law. Hence B. Reicke, *Glaube und Leben*, pp. 124ff., several times rightly lays stress on 'radically nationalistic proceedings against Stephen'; but he does not investigate thoroughly the problem as to the attitude of Stephen which would have provoked the murderous hatred of the 'nationalists'.

especially as Galilee was the home of the first Christians. Matt. 5.18 is altogether unique in the earliest Christian writings. Unlike the Pharisees, not even the primitive Church considered the Law to be the road to salvation. The reason for the division into Hebrews and Hellenists, and the consequent different treatment as regards persecution by the Jews can therefore hardly have lain in the greater or lesser extent to which the Law was observed by the two groups. Haenchen, too, has recognized this in the new edition of his commentary.[36]

The Hellenists' criticism of the Law must have been fundamental in character and struck at the foundations of Jewish existence, if an explanation is to be found for the division in the primitive Church and for the bloody persecution of the Hellenists. Thus Klein thinks that 'what the Hellenists took for granted in their activities described in 11.19 and what made them effective must be also applied already to the Jerusalem period.'[36a] Accordingly he sees 'in their avowal of a mission to the Gentiles unfettered by the Law their fundamental heresy in Jewish and "Hebrew" Christian eyes'. This brings our problem nearer to solution, but does not solve it entirely. What G. Klein has recognized is basically correct, but must be examined more thoroughly.

When we observe that the Jerusalem church gave the hand of fellowship through its leaders to the apostle Paul, expressly in view of his Gentile mission which disregarded the Law (Gal. 2.9), we shall have to ask whether, in fact, in the earlier period a different attitude prevailed.[37] We may reply that the so-called

[36] 13th ed., p. 221.
[36a] 'Besprechung', pp. 362ff.
[37] So also Haenchen, 13th ed., p. 221. He now thinks correctly that 'what roused the Jews in Jerusalem against Stephen's party can really only have lain in the great freedom with which they regard the Law' (*loc. cit.*) Thus he accepts Klein's well-founded criticism of his treatment of our problem in the 10th edition (the first revised by him) of Meyer's Commentary on the Acts, and at the same time he rejects (correctly, but on insufficient grounds) Klein's thesis concerning the Gentile mission propagated by the Hellenists in Jerusalem. But then Haenchen's own exegesis breaks down, too. He recalls Jesus' freedom with regard to questions of the sabbath and cleanliness and thinks that perhaps the 'Hellenists' had interpreted the Law more nearly in Jesus' sense than the 'Hebrews'. But, in the first place, the synoptic accounts of Jesus' lax views of the Law undoubtedly reflect the approach of the primitive Palestinian church as a whole, and so of the 'Hebrews' in particular (see p. 37 n. 81). And besides, this lax approach is unusual only when compared with the strictness of the Pharisaic teaching, but not when compared with the practical approach of the mass of the *am haaretz* in Palestine. Thus such freedom as regards the Law could never have supplied a reason for bloody persecution. Consequently the 'Hellenists' must have dared to claim a *greater* freedom from the Law.

apostolic council came into being as a result of the pressure of circumstances which had been created in the meantime and signified an abandonment of the older Jerusalem principle which placed the Gentiles, too, under the Law.[38] That may be, but it cannot be proved and is, as we shall see later, extremely improbable. It is in any case precarious to support our proof by Matt. 10.5f., 23; 8.5–10; Mark 7.24–30—we shall return to these passages —because these traditions cannot be assigned to a particular place. On the other hand, Paul declares emphatically that the churches in Judea from the start of his activities glorified God because of the gospel which he preached, which, of course, dissociated itself from the Law (Gal. 1.23f.). Where could time still be found for the Christians in Judea to have taken up originally an attitude rejecting such a gospel? It is therefore extremely doubtful whether a division could arise in the original Jerusalem church merely on account of the Gentile mission which disregarded the Law.

Moreover, it is most improbable that the problem of a Gentile mission dissociated from the Law could arise precisely in Jerusalem; and even more improbable that there could establish itself in that very city a group in the Church whose special theological concern it was to preach to the Gentiles a gospel dissociated from the Law, which attracted attention by this peculiarity and provoked a deadly anger. This problem is at home in the Diaspora, and to this extent Luke is quite correct in making the Hellenists' mission to the Gentiles begin first in Antioch. Jerusalem was the most disadvantageous point of departure imaginable for the mission to the Gentiles which disregarded the Law.

But it is especially difficult to believe that the Jews killed Stephen because he did not impose the *Jewish* Law on a *Gentile* who became a *Christian*. The existence of the Jews is not affected if Gentiles, when they became Christians, could live in exactly the same freedom from the Law as before. Later on, too, the 'original church' certainly ran no risk of being persecuted by the Jews merely because it declared its agreement with Paul's mission to the Gentiles which claimed independence from the Law (Gal. 2.1–10). Such a mission did not as yet question the validity of the Law for Jews. Nor is there any evidence that the Jews took steps against

[38] So Klein now in respect of the discussion of Haenchen's 13th edition in ZKG 73, 1962, p. 360.

the Christian mission to the Gentiles as such.[39] What did it matter to the pious Jew if the Christians invited the Gentiles into a kingdom of which the Lord was the crucified Jesus of Nazareth? His kingdom was certainly not the Kingdom of God they expected.

Klein's thesis must therefore be expanded so far as to make it clear that Stephen and his group declared the Law as a whole, including circumcision, to be abolished both for Jews and for Jewish Christians, as Paul also did.[40] This necessarily led to a division in the Jerusalem church. For even if the 'Hebrews' could have joined in taking the step to freedom from the Law *theologically*, they were obliged merely for the sake of their own safety to cling to the Law. For the persecution of the Hellenists showed clearly how the Jews were obliged to reply to the challenge of those fellow countrymen who rejected the Law as a whole and thereby denied not only Israel's special relationship with God[41] but also risked their national existence; for the 'Law' was also undoubtedly the foundation of Jewish self-government in Palestine. 'Membership of the Jewish nation required the observance of particular

---

[39] This did not prevent all sorts of difficulties from being made for the apostate Paul in his Gentile mission. Admittedly I Thess. 2.15 has been seriously suspected of being a gloss (cf. commentaries). Yet Gal. 5.11; 6.12 must also be compared. It can hardly have been agreeable to the synagogue that the Pauline mission obviously liked to get in touch with Gentiles who as 'God-fearers' stood already in a loose relationship to Judaism (see pp. 61f.). For now the fruits laboriously cultivated by Jewish propaganda fell as an easy prey into the lap of the Christians when they then refrained from placing the heavy yoke of the Law on the 'God-fearers' ' neck before making them full members of their community. This behaviour must have appeared to the Jews to be a device as adroit as it was mean. It is difficult to overestimate the extent of the missionary efforts of the synagogue and therefore it is impossible to doubt the missionary concern of Jewry during the period before the year 70 (see p. 61). Hence altercations between Paul and the Jews were inevitable. P. H. Menoud, L'*église naissante et le Judaïsme* (Etudes théologiques et religieuses 27), 1952, pp. 1–52, points out, perhaps correctly, that the Jews could have had no interest in letting the Christians share in the protection granted to their religion. It was just because they did not recognize the (Gentile) Christians as Jews that they accused them to the Roman authorities. That Paul was exposed to trouble from the Jews is also due, apart from his missionary activity, to the fact that he was an apostate.

[40] Actually the step to take to the Gentiles a gospel dissociated from the Law included taking that same gospel to the Jews as well—and *vice versa*. For if access had been opened up through faith in Christ to the Gentiles, who had no Law, it was impossible any longer to impose the Law on Jewish Christians as the means of salvation. And if the Kingdom of God came to the Jews who ignored the Law, the Gentile who did the same could hardly be excluded from this Kingdom.

[41] 'Our Lawgiver . . . fenced us round with impregnable ramparts and walls of iron, that we might not mingle at all with any of the other nations, but remain pure in body and soul, free from all vain imaginations, worshipping the one Almighty God above the whole creation' (Letter of Aristeas 139).

regulations and customs.'[42] The persecution of Hellenists who were not bound by the Law was therefore an absolutely necessary act of national and religious self-defence.

The fact that the Hebrews remained unmolested shows the possibility of bad Jews, too, living in Jerusalem.[43] Only they were not allowed to cut the ground away from under the feet of Jewry.[44]

It is worth while to return once more to the terms 'Ἑβραῖοι—Ἑλληνισταί. It has become sufficiently clear that in the circumstances described in Acts 6ff. they cannot primarily denote differences of language. But Cadbury's theory that the word 'Hellenist' is intended to denote Gentile Christians is also improbable. The earlier, the more likely it was that Hellenist *Jewish* Christians, especially in Jerusalem, must have been pioneers for freedom from the control of the Law. So it is most probable that special attention is drawn to Nicolaus as a proselyte amongst the seven leaders of the Hellenist community, because he was the only one of them who was a Gentile by birth.

In the New Testament period Ἑβραῖος is the name of the genuine Jew who is aware of his intimate bond with the traditions of his fathers, his national and his Palestinian home,[45] even though he speaks the Greek language. Ἑβραῖος is a 'pure-blooded Jew';[46] yet the term Ἑβραῖος does not by itself make it clear in what sense to be a Jew is understood. Even Paul calls himself a 'Hebrew' in a particular situation (Phil. 3.5; II Cor. 11.22)!

Corresponding to this, a Ἑλληνιστής is a man who knows that

---

[42] G. Strecker, 'Christentum', p. 462.

[43] There is nothing to suggest that amongst the 'Hebrews' an actual separate Jerusalem group under James and a similar Galilean one under Peter could be discerned, as W. Grundmann supposes in *ZNW* 38, 1939, p. 54.

[44] I will cite Haenchen once again from the revised edition of his commentary on the Acts: 'However this may be, in any case, this principle in the preaching of the "Hellenists" must have appeared strange and alarming not only to the Jews, but to the "Hebrews" (for the fact that they were not persecuted shows that they had not accepted this principle)' (13th ed., p. 221). He means the principle which criticizes the Law. Haenchen does not undertake a more exact definition of it. Would he admit the only possible conclusion from the above true comment to be that the Hellenists in Jerusalem must be antinomians like, for example, Paul, if the radical division in the primitive church in Jerusalem and the bloody persecution of the Hellenists is to be made intelligible?

[45] Cadbury, 'The Hellenists', pp. 62ff.; W. Gutbrod in *TWNT* III, 374ff., 392ff.; T. Hopfner, 'Die Judenfrage bei Griechen und Römern', *Abhandlung der Akademie der Wissenschaften zu Prag* 8, 1940, p. 30.

[46] H. Lietzmann, *Korinther*, on II Cor. 11.22.

he is commited to the Greek way of life, whether he is a Jew by birth or even an Aramaic-speaking Jew. The word is derived from ἑλληνίζειν = to live like a Greek; its particular meaning is determined in each case by the term with which it is contrasted. It is intended to denote, not national characteristics or language especially, but a way of life as a whole.⁴⁷ Thus some later writers call those Greeks who have remained pagan Ἑλληνισταί as contrasted with Christians.⁴⁸ In Acts 9.29 the Ἑλληνισταί are the Jews of the Diaspora contrasted with Palestinian Jews; in Acts 11.20 they are Greeks contrasted with Jews in general. When in Acts 6.1 a distinction is made amongst the Christians between Ἑβραῖοι and Ἑλληνισταί, then in view of the meaning of Ἑβραῖοι, which can be perceived clearly from the context in Acts 6ff. to be Jewish Christians who observe the Law, the Ἑλληνισταί can only be understood to be un-'Hebrew', i.e. living in the Greek way; and thus here Christians living free from the control of the Law, whether they were Jewish or Greek by origin and language. This was the explanation of the expression in Acts 6.1 given by G. P. Wetter.⁴⁹ It is possible that this word was coined for the first time as a technical term for the Christians who were free from the control of the Law, as G. P. Wetter conjectures.⁵⁰

Thus the pair of opposites Ἑβραῖοι–Ἑλληνισταί already allows us to infer that the Hellenists had an un-Jewish attitude, which in view of their being persecuted, proved itself to be pronounced antinomianism.

Accordingly behind the Lucan formulation that Stephen speaks words against the Temple and the Law (Acts 6.14) there lies concealed the antinomianism of Stephen's theological position. It seems that Luke knew this also quite well, for in Acts 21.28 he makes the Jews bring up the same accusations against Paul as they had raised in Acts 6.13 against Stephen, and it is only with difficulty that Paul escapes the threat of Stephen's fate. The wording of the

---

⁴⁷ Cadbury, p. 60; H. Windisch in *TWNT* II, 508; O. Cullmann, *The Christology of the New Testament*, ET 1957, p. 165 n. 1. The contrasted term is ἰουδαΐζειν.

⁴⁸ Cadbury, p. 59; Windisch in *TWNT* II, 509.

⁴⁹ G. P. Wetter, pp. 410ff.; cf. also O. Cullmann, 'The Significance of the Qumran Texts for Research in the Beginnings of Christianity', *JBL* 74, 1955, pp. 220f., reprinted in *The Scrolls and the New Testament*, ed. Krister Stendahl, 1958, pp. 25ff.; W. Bauer, 'Jesus der Galiläer' in *Festgabe für A. Jülicher*, pp. 32f.; but particularly in M. Simon, *Stephen*, pp. 12f.; Windisch in *TWNT* II, 508f.

⁵⁰ Cf. also Cadbury, p. 70.

account of Paul's arrest, especially v. 28, must, like 6.13, be assigned to Luke.[51] It is in essentials the same. But in the story of Paul's arrival in Jerusalem Luke hands down to us on the basis of a good source[52] the meaning of this accusation against Paul. According to Acts 21.21 the Jewish (Christians) had been told about Paul, and Paul learns through the Christians of Jerusalem 'that you teach all the Jews who are among the Gentiles to forsake Moses, telling them not to circumcise their children or observe the (Jewish) customs.'

Since Luke repeats this clear accusation of antinomianism in 21.28 with the same words with which he describes the Jewish reproaches against Stephen, he may also in the case of the latter have been aware of his real position.

If anyone should call in question the existence and activity in the earliest period of Christianity of such antinomianism,[53] we will merely point here to the indisputable fact that Paul before his conversion persecuted the Christians, and did so just because of his zeal for the Law. His conversion, as Gal. 1.13ff. shows, was a conversion to the gospel which he had persecuted, the gospel free from the Law. Thus this gospel existed already in early days outside Jerusalem,[54] and it was, in fact, a gospel which placed the *Jew*, too, apart from the Law; for it was as a Jew that Paul gave up obedience to the Law, owing to his conversion. Moreover, it may have been Luke who fitted in Stephen's story just at this point of time when he needed it (see below). It might, in fact, have occurred later than Paul's conversion.

But how could such a separate group *come into being* in Jerusalem? Obviously not at all! If there were during the New Testament period any city which might be regarded as the very last place where Christian freedom from the control of the Law could arise, then it is Jerusalem. This applies, in whatever way the Hellenism of the Ἑλληνισταί is defined in detail.[55] The original

[51] Haenchen, pp. 551f./546ff.
[52] See pp. 86ff.
[53] W. G. Kümmel in *TR* 17, 1948–9, p. 22f., also allows rightly for a Hellenistic community *before* Stephen.
[54] Cf. R. Bultmann, in *Glauben und Verstehen* I, p. 189; W. Schrage, 'Ekklesia und Synagoge', *ZTK* 60, 1963, pp. 197f.
[55] G. P. Wetter (*ARW* 21, pp. 412f. *et passim*), who thinks that the Hellenists are predominantly Gentile Christians, considers that Luke's source began with a narrative about the founding of *the two* Christian churches in Jerusalem, but without asking how a Gentile-Christian church could come to be founded just in *Jerusalem*.

Hellenist Christianity did not arise in Jerusalem,[56] but in the

---

W. Grundmann follows Wetter in recognizing the difficulty concealed in this problem and clearly allows for a larger number of Gentile inhabitants in Jerusalem (*ZNW* 38, 1939, p. 57). That is extremely unlikely. For a criticism of Grundmann on other points see Kümmel in *TR* 17, 1948, pp. 23ff. We need only reflect that it seems to have been the Hellenistic Jews of Jerusalem (Acts 6.9) who murdered Stephen. Hence how far even from them must Stephen's theological position have been.

Cadbury ('The Hellenists', p. 69) agrees with Grundmann in his picture of the development. But he also considers the possibility that Luke may have transferred conditions of his own time into the narrative about Stephen.

Lastly W. Bauer ('Jesus der Galiläer', pp. 32f.) assumes that the 'Hellenists' come from Galilee. That is possible, although I conjecture a more direct place of origin elsewhere (see below). But at any rate Bauer was right in seeing that the 'Hellenists' must have come from outside Jerusalem, in fact from a Gentile environment which had no Law.

[56] Of course, there were Hellenistic synagogues in Jerusalem, too, which as such undoubtedly pioneered the way for a Christianity free from control of the Law. For there are signs especially in Hellenistic Judaism of a more independent attitude to the Law, even to circumcision. Rabbi Meir (*c.* 150) is said to have remarked several times that a non-Jew who observes the Torah would receive a reward, namely by *carrying out* the commandments (*BQ* 38a; *San*, 586 and *passim*; see Billerbeck I, 362f.; III, 79). Rabbi Jehoshua declared that a baptized man must be considered a proselyte according to the general, that is ancient, opinion, even if he was not circumcised. (*Jeb.* 46a = Billerbeck I, pp. 106f.) Cf. *Orac. Sib.* IV 162ff., and on this Billerbeck I, p. 106.

Josephus records that King Izates of Adiabene, who was first converted to Judaism on the advice of his teacher, the merchant Ananias, omitted circumcision. 'He said that he was able even without circumcision τὸ θεῖον σέβειν, εἴγε πάντως κέκρικε ζηλοῦν τὰ πάτρια τῶν Ἰουδαίων. τοῦτ' εἶναι κυριώτερον τοῦ περιτέμνεσθαι.' Yet later he is circumcised after all at the suggestion of a Galilean teacher who held strictly to the Law (Jos. *Ant.* XX 2.4).

Philo (*De migr. Abr.* 89ff.) objects to those who pursue the allegorical interpretation of the Law with such fervour that they neglect the actual meaning of the words. He declares with regard to them that ordinances about the sabbath and the feast days, the rule about circumcision and the regulations about the Temple worship, must be obeyed literally as well. 'For if they are observed correctly, that for which they are symbols will also be perceived more clearly, apart from the fact that many peoples' accusations and reproaches will be avoided.'

Three times we find in Paul's writings in different forms the principle 'neither circumcision counts for anything nor uncircumcision, but keeping the commandments of God' (I Cor. 7.19; Gal. 5.6, 6.15; cf. Rom. 2.26). Obviously this principle originated in the Hellenistic synagogue. According to a scholium on Gal. 6.15 (see HNT *ad loc.*) it is said to have been found, too, in an apocryphal writing of Moses. Cf. also P. Dalbert, *Missionsliteratur*, pp. 16, 65.

It is not really likely that the Hellenistic synagogues *in Jerusalem* had such liberal ideas. But even if they had, the antinomianism of the circle of Stephen (and of Paul) differs altogether from a certain diffidence in some Jewish circles with regard to carrying out circumcision understood as an *opus operatum*. When a Hellenistic Jew said that what mattered was not the act of circumcision but keeping God's commandment, this did not thereby call in question Israel's exclusive relationship to God. It only meant that this relationship was established less by means of circumcision than by observance of the moral commandments of God's people. When Stephen or Paul say that circumcision and uncircumcision count for nothing, it signifies that Israel has no longer any religious privilege. Israel's exclusive relation is impugned. Therefore, instead of 'keeping the commandments of God' (I Cor. 7.19), Paul can speak of

Hellenistic world; perhaps its origin was connected with a mission to the Gentiles. We do not know for certain where to look for the origin of the church in Jerusalem led by Stephen and the Seven which dissociated itself from the Law. The Syrian area around Antioch might be assumed (see below).[57] That these Hellenists quite early formed themselves into a church in Jerusalem, too, is most simply explained by the same reason which also brought to Jerusalem even earlier the 'Hebrews', whose home was in Galilee. It was in Jerusalem that the imminent parousia was espected.[58]

4. The hypothesis that the Hellenistic Christianity of Jerusalem did not originate in Jerusalem itself does indeed conflict with Luke's account, according to which the Christian message first crossed the boundaries of the city of Jerusalem in consequence of the persecution aroused by Stephen's death and reached Judea,

---

'faith' (Gal. 5.6) or of the 'new creation' (Gal. 6.15) as the realities by which circumcision has been replaced.

The fundamental abolition of Israel's special privilege which this implies could not happen in an entirely Jewish environment, but only in the Gentile world. Not much light can as yet be thrown on the obscurity surrounding the beginnings of this antinomianism. Some preparation had indeed perhaps been made in certain Hellenistic circles which gave priority to the moral precept over the demand for circumcision; but still this does not explain what is really new, namely the denial that Israel is God's people in a unique way. Is this the theological achievement of a particular primitive Christian personality? This is unlikely. At any rate, Paul found already in existence this antinomianism which he persecuted. I should like to conjecture here foreign influences in the region of Antioch, in which antinomianism is at home (see below and Schmithals, *Apostelamt*, pp. 187ff.).

[57] I can see no reason for seeking the immediate origin of the Hellenists among the Essenes (O. Cullmann, 'The Significance of the Qumran Texts for Research into the Beginnings of Christianity', *JBL* 74, 1955, pp. 213–26 = *The Scrolls and the New Testament*, 1958, pp. 18–32; cautiously also J. Daniélou in *Les manuscrits de la Mer Morte et les origines du christianisme* (1957; ET, *The Dead Sea Scrolls and Primitive Christianity*, Baltimore, 1958), ch. III, section 1. The Qumran group were rigorous defenders of the Law, and to that extent far removed from ἑλληνίζειν. Cf. Haenchen, 13th ed., pp. 214ff., who also criticizes other matters in Cullmann. Certain points of contact are no evidence of dependence, but are explained by their common milieu of oriental syncretism. Cullmann carries his thesis further in 'L'Opposition contre le Temple de Jérusalem, Motif Commun de la Théologie Johannique et du Monde Ambiant', *NTS* 5, 1959, pp. 157–73. Cf. also P. Geoltrain, 'Esséniens et Hellénistes', *TZ* 15, 1959, pp. 241–54; A. F. J. Klijn, 'Stephen's speech, Acts 7.2–53', *NTS* 4, 1957, pp. 25ff.

[58] Of course, it is only natural, even in the absence of this purposive theological motive, that Christians who had that bias against the control of the Law should for the most varied personal reasons go to Jerusalem and combine to form a community there. Jerusalem was the Jewish capital city with which the Jews were connected by all kinds of links. Similarly Christians, in fact, meet together in Rome, too, brought to the capital of the empire by multifarious reasons, but hardly by a planned mission, and build up a church there.

Samaria, Galilee(!) and finally Antioch (Acts 8.1, 4f.; 11.19). The historicity of this presentation of the events[59] was asserted with all the more confidence, since the conviction prevailed that we had in Acts 11.19–30 an original ('Antiochian') report which followed on immediately after 8.4.[60] But what O. Bauernfeind[61] had already pointed out, has been established by Haenchen,[62] namely, that we have in 11.19–30 a typical Lucan summary.[63]

Luke naturally uses for it old traditions from Antioch. We can quite confidently assign to these traditions the names of the earliest prophets and teachers from Antioch which occur in Acts 13.1.[63a] Luke knew from Barnabas that he was a Cypriot (Acts 4.36) and that Lucius came from Cyrene (13.1). He puts this together in 11.20 and states that some of those who were persecuted in Jerusalem, men of Cyprus and Cyrene, brought the gospel to Antioch. But the names in 13.1 have nothing to do with those in Acts 6.5. The statement in 11.20 that the persons named in 13.1 were refugees from Jerusalem is made up by Luke.[64] In fact, no trace of a source can be discovered which connects 11.19ff. with 8.4.

The obvious tension between Acts 11.19ff. and the story about

---

[59] It has not been disputed by G. P. Wetter or W. Grundmann either; both make Gentile Christianity originate in Jerusalem!

[60] A. von Harnack, *The Acts of the Apostles*, ET (New Testament Studies 3), 1909, p. 199; W. Grundmann in *ZNW* 38, 1939, pp. 54f.; J. Jeremias, 'Untersuchungen zum Quellenproblem der Apostelgeschichte', *ZNW* 36, 1937, pp. 205–21; H. H. Wendt, 'Die Hauptquelle der Apostelgeschichte', *ZNW* 24, 1925, pp. 293ff.

[61] O. Bauernfeind, *Die Apostelgeschichte*, p. 153.

[62] Pp. 320/313f.

[63] In my opinion we must adhere at all costs to this finding. R. Bultmann's renewed defence (in *New Testament Essays*, studies in memory of T. W. Manson, edited by A. J. B. Higgins, Manchester, 1959, pp. 68–80) of a continuous source from Antioch linking Acts 8.4a with 11.19 seems to me to be insufficiently substantiated; cf. also Haenchen, 13th ed., pp. 75f.

[63a] Dibelius, *Acts*, p. 17 n. 3.

[64] We do indeed meet with Barnabas in Jerusalem in Acts 4.36f. But it is in the tradition of Antioch alone that he is anchored *firmly*, and E. Schwartz long ago made the correct conjecture (*NGG*, 1907, p. 282 n. 1) that that first report about Barnabas is derived from the prototype used for 13.1ff. and was first transferred to Jerusalem by Luke. This would enable the impossible interpretation of the name Barnabas as the 'Son of consolation' to be explained; namely, Luke had in error applied to Barnabas a note about Manaen (= Menahem, in II Kings 15.14 = consoler).

Luke needed the Hellenist Barnabas to be in Jerusalem in the first instance, in order to let the Gentile mission in Antioch receive the sanction of the apostolic authority controlling the Church (Haenchen, pp. 321f./314f.). The account in Acts 9.27 which is historically impossible (Haenchen, pp. 289f./282f.) shows him to be the suitable man for the purpose.

Cornelius justifies us in considering the tradition that Antioch is the home of freedom from the control of the Law, that very same freedom of which the Hellenist church in Jerusalem was the victim, to be genuine also. Therefore the beginnings of the church in Antioch placed by Luke at the time of 11.19ff. were earlier than Stephen's martyrdom. The fact that at least one of the leaders of the Hellenist church in Jerusalem, namely Nicolaus, came from Antioch builds a bridge from Antioch to Jerusalem, not the other way round, even though members of Stephen's circle may after his martyrdom have attached themselves to the mother church in Antioch.

This view of things is supported also by the fact that in the early days of the Church Paul must have been active as a persecutor of the Christians who ignored the Law in the regions of Syria and Cilicia, contrary to the account in Acts (cf. Gal. 1.21); for he declared emphatically that he was personally unknown to the churches in Judea (Gal. 1.22). Of course, Luke was obliged to transfer Paul's persecuting activities to Judea, if only because according to the narrative of Acts Christianity had not yet reached Antioch and its neighbourhood at the time of Paul's conversion.

Now we can perceive also what lay behind Luke's description of the events concerning Stephen. It is only from hints that we learned from Luke that the church in Jerusalem was seriously divided, that Stephen came forward as an antinomian, that only part of the church was persecuted. Luke himself makes it behave with great unanimity and so be persecuted collectively, too, and he also produces false witnesses for the accusation against Stephen. Why?

An important underlying trend of Luke's delineation of the history appears in his endeavour to present Jerusalem consistently as the headquarters of Christianity, from which all its developments emanate or at least receive their sanction, to whose authority all Christendom, even Pauline Christendom, is subject.[65] Luke presents this picture consistently, at any rate so far as the data

[65] The motives for this most conspicuous tendency in Luke's reporting of events, which G. Klein, *Die Zwölf Apostel*, has recently brought out emphatically, need not be examined here. Certainly Luke's endeavour to prove Christianity to be the true Judaism springs from the same purpose. Haenchen conjectures apologetic motives: Christianity is to be recognized 'as an internal Jewish αἵρεσις, hence as a *religio licita*' (pp. 565/560). This has already been maintained by H. J. Holtzmann (*Die Apostelgeschichte*, p. 17). But see pp. 57ff.

permit. Thus Galilee is already cut out of the Easter narratives in his Gospel.[66] The whole Christian church lives from the beginning in Jerusalem. From there it spreads to Judea, Samaria (8.1) and finally to Galilee as well (9.31) and beyond. Haenchen affirms correctly that Luke 'apparently had no material'[67] about the Christianization of Galilee. Indeed, how could he have had it! This material is, after all, not suitable for Acts, but is already contained in the gospel.[68] Not Jerusalem, but Galilee is the home of Christianity.[69] It is certain that very soon the Church shifted its centre to Jerusalem, where it expected the parousia of him who was crucified there.[70] But, of course, an original church remained

---

[66] W. Marxsen, *Der Evangelist Markus* (FRLANT 67), 1956, pp. 47ff., has declared—following the example of others—this conception of the Easter events to be the historically correct one. In his view the disciples certainly did not return to Galilee after Jesus' death. The passages in Mark, Matthew and John which maintain this are all said to be editorial interpolations of the evangelist Mark. I Cor. 15 knows nothing about Galilee. I do not think that there is anything to justify this theory. All earlier traces of the resurrection stories point to Galilee, and there is little likelihood of the group of Jesus' adherents having remained in Judea after his execution. They certainly had not cut all links with their home when they set out for Jerusalem for the Passover. But even if they had done so, as W. Marxsen assumes, yet a group of Jesus' adherents would have remained behind in Galilee. It is just this which conflicts with Luke's description.

[67] Pp. 287/280.

[68] The synoptic material still awaits interpretation with the spread of Christianity in Galilee in the post-Easter period in mind.

[69] It must be recalled that this was already asserted by R. Schütz, *Apostel und Jünger*, 1921. He starts from a stark antagonism between Paul and James. Here he is in error. His study has been rightly rejected, especially on account of his impossible division of the sources in Acts. He reconstructs an apostles' source and a disciples' source, the former Judaistic, the latter Hellenistic. The results of his work are based on this thesis. But although the solution of the problem which Schütz has seen may be quite impossible, the problem itself, owing to the rejection of his solution, still persists. Hence the introduction to his study remains worth reading, for he points out that already in the early beginnings of Christianity the existence of Jewish-Christian and Hellenistic elements side by side can be established. And it is still worth while to read the conclusion (pp. 94-107), which, with whatever reservations it may be read, says much that is true about the significance of Galilee in the history of primitive Christianity, which has been much neglected by recent research following Luke's example.

The question we have posed is also suggested to a certain extent in C. C. Torrey's essay, 'The Aramaic Period of the Nascent Christian Church', *ZNW* 44, 1952/3, pp. 205-23. Cf. also L. E. Elliott-Binns, *Galilean Christianity* (SBT 16), 1956, especially pp. 43ff.; in spite of many bad arguments he is right in recognizing the significance of Galilee for early Christianity.

[70] Perhaps Jerusalem, too, as K. Holl conjectures, soon developed with the self-assurance of its inhabitants to be the official headquarters of Christianity as a whole. On the other hand, we ought not to overestimate the significance of Jerusalem in the *very early* period. We possess, for instance, no reliable information which might suggest to us that the circle of the Twelve made their home even temporarily in Jerusalem.

active in Galilee⁷¹ and disseminated its influence not only to Jerusalem by way of Samaria, but also to Syria, Damascus, Antioch, all places where the Acts takes early Christian churches for granted.⁷² The religious and political connexions of 'Galilee of the Gentiles'⁷³ were at least as close to the north as to the south.

[71] The problems upon which we have touched are dealt with also by E. Lohmeyer in his well-known book, *Galiläa und Jerusalem* (FRLANT 52), 1936, as well as elsewhere, especially in the essay, 'Das Abendmahl in der Urgemeinde', *JBL* 56, 1937, pp. 217–52. Lohmeyer realizes correctly that there must have existed a church in Galilee when the history of the Church began. But he is already mistaken in speaking of two original churches. He must speak either of one original church, which in that case would be the Galilean one, or of several, in which case alongside the mother church in Galilee the daughter churches in Jerusalem and Judea, in Antioch, in Damascus and Syria, in Samaria and perhaps elsewhere would stand as regards their origin—not their importance—essentially on the same level. It is still more erroneous to assign to the mistakenly conjectured two original churches separate theological ideologies. We are, of course, justified theoretically in allowing for local theological peculiarities, but in that case we cannot make do with only two localities possessing original churches.

If we wish nevertheless to speak of two original churches in the early period, it can only be done if we suppose that, in addition to the churches imbued with the Easter faith who confessed Jesus as Christ, there remained in Galilee to start with and for some time active churches who in imitation of the historical Jesus were expecting not Jesus as the Son of Man but the coming of God in his heavenly Kingdom. So far as I know these churches have not yet been taken into account by historical research, to the great disadvantage of all efforts to elucidate the beginnings of Christianity and the origins of the synoptic tradition.

It is a separate question whether the early spread of the gospel from Galilee in the most diverse directions presuppose a conscious mission, and thus real missionaries. This presupposition is not actually necessary. Eschatological movements are often apt to spread very fast. But I should like to draw attention to the fact that Paul, according to Gal. 1.17ff., presupposes 'apostles' in Jerusalem at the time of his conversion. There is discussion about the particular people who are to be counted as 'apostles'. But there should be none about the fact that the *concept* of apostle used here is the Pauline one, according to which the apostle is an envoy appointed by Christ to spread the gospel. Paul knows no kind of apostle other than this (if we disregard the non-theological use of the apostle concept in the case of the 'messengers of the churches' in II Cor. 8.23; Phil. 2.25). Three years after Paul's conversion the majority of the apostles are, in fact, on journeys—presumably on active service (Gal. 1.19). This can, after all, only be understood on the supposition that at latest at the time of Paul's conversion, and that means practically from the beginning of the Church, a Christian mission was in existence. It must not be objected that this runs counter to all that we know about Judaism. Admitted! (Yet cf. Matt. 23.15 and J. Jeremias, *Jesus' Promise to the Nations*, ET (SBT 24), 1958, pp. 11–19.) But the home of Christianity is not Jerusalem nor orthodox Judaism, but 'Galilee of the Gentiles', permeated by syncretism. Moreover, the concept 'mission' is capable of being charged with a great variety of particular meanings and must not be seen directly in the light of Paul's missionary methods; cf. also pp. 61f. below. Yet the synoptic tradition is aware of not a few logia which presuppose a planned mission of Jewish-Christian missionaries in the early period; cf. also I Cor. 9.5 and see below, pp. 111f.

[72] See W. G. Kümmel in *TR* 17, 1948–9, pp. 18f.

[73] For the spread of paganism in Galilee cf. L. E. Elliott-Binns, *Galilean Christianity*, pp. 17ff. Cf. also M. Dibelius, *Die Formgeschichte des Evangeliums*³, 1959, pp. 27ff.; G. Schrenk, *Galiläa zur Zeit Jesu* (Jugend und Evangelium 7), Basel, 1941.

Otherwise it would be impossible to understand not only the whole affair about Stephen but also Paul and his conversion to the Christianity free from Law which he had hitherto persecuted. Mark is right in regarding Galilee as the Holy Land[74] and the synoptic tradition is anchored essentially in Galilee and its surroundings not only on account of its origin but also from the point of view of the history of its tradition.[75] The mission of the Lord's brothers, attested by Paul in I Cor. 9.5, might have had its home in Galilee.

Even Luke, too, could not ignore the fact that Paul had been active in early days as a persecutor, since the conversion of Paul took place near Damascus, an event which had stamped itself upon the consciousness of Christianity. Luke—presumably contrary to the historical course of events—makes the conversion of Paul come after the persecution of Stephen and sends Paul to Damascus in order to find out whether the new teaching had already spread so far in the short time after Stephen's death; in this way he succeeds in avoiding the difficulty which this involves. But in doing so he has to accept the supposition that the Christians are at first allowed to go free, and must then be pursued as far as Damascus, where in any case the Jerusalem authorities no longer possessed any jurisdiction. Actually the fact of Paul's activity as a persecutor in the Damascus area shows that Christianity did not first leave the walls of Jerusalem after Stephen's persecution and advance gradually from Judea to Syria, but that it had already reached Syria at an early period and in fact apparently from Galilee.

These considerations are sufficient to wreck Luke's design, which is what determines his presentation of Stephen's martyrdom. Luke could not give up this story. It gave him the golden opportunity to account for the Christian mission, for the passage of the gospel beyond the bounds of Jerusalem, and even to lay it at the door of the Jewish authorities (disliked by the Romans also).[76] The Christian Church, living in complete concord with the Temple, the nation and the Law, would never on its own account

---

[74] See Kümmel, *TR* 17, 1948–9, pp. 17f. Cf. W. Marxsen, *Der Evangelist Markus*, pp. 33ff., who, in fact, looks for the *Sitz im Leben* of Mark's Galilee tradition in the circumstances of the Church at the time of Mark.

[75] So it is not a matter for surprise that οἱ Γαλιλαῖοι is attested several times as an early name of the Christians; see the passages in E. Peterson, *Frühkirche, Judentum und Gnosis*, 1959, pp. 64f., and Epict. IV 7, 6.

[76] Cf. J. Weiss, pp. 11f.

have thought of such an enterprise![77] Since Stephen had first to be introduced as an important figure in the primitive Church beside the apostles, who up till then had alone dominated the scene, Luke simply could not omit the account of the division in the Church in Acts 6.1–7.

The true reason for this division, and therefore also Stephen's real attitude and the motive for his death as a martyr, and hence, too, what actually happened during the persecution, must be suppressed by Luke, although his account reveals that he knew more about it than he tells.[78] For otherwise he would have had to explain how a Jewish-Christian church which disregarded the Law could come into being amongst the presuppositions of the early Christians of Jerusalem, who according to Luke's account observed the Law strictly; that is to say, in practice he would have had to give up the fiction that Stephen was really the cause of the world-wide mission, whereas he was, in fact, a victim of Christian antinomianism which had long been active beyond the Jewish frontiers.[79] Luke would thus have had to relinquish the essential purpose of his book, which was to make Jerusalem the undisputed point of departure and the centre of the history of the Church.[80]

That he was unable to achieve this explains his treatment of the tradition concerning Stephen.

The preceding discussion is intended to introduce us to the problem of the relationship between Paul and James. We will sum up its results: There was already in the early days in Jerusalem a party amongst the primitive Christians who observed the Law,

---

[77] If we notice the role which the Stephen narrative *must* play at this precise point in Luke's account, we shall beware of following Luke's dating too confidently. When Paul was in Jerusalem for the 'Apostolic Council' the persecution may, in fact, have lain already sometime back in the past, but I Thess. 2.14 may be alluding to it; cf. H. J. Schoeps, *Urgemeinde*, p. 14.

[78] See p. 27.

[79] When it comes to describing Paul's arrest in Jerusalem these considerations are, of course dropped. Thus Luke can without any scruples let the antinomian form of the accusations against Paul in Acts 21.21 stand beside his more moderate version of them in Acts 21.28.

[80] Schoeps accepts Luke's picture of primitive Christianity as his viewpoint of its history and makes Paul into the first Hellenist Christian. It is probably for this reason that he perceives with greater perspicacity than any other commentator that the story about Stephen is a foreign element within Luke's presentation which upsets it completely. His 'solution' of this difficulty consists in regarding the Hellenists as an association based on local affiliations elsewhere, and in supposing the figure of Stephen to have been invented by Luke (*Theologie*, pp. 440f.; *Urgemeinde*, pp. 5f., 13). But whatever criticisms may be raised against the account in the Acts, it must not be overlooked that Luke is using existing traditions for the story about Stephen.

and another which was free from its control. The two were organized separately, which was indeed required by their different attitudes to the Law. We cannot be sure what their relation to each other was like. We can hardly assume that they faced each other with actual hostility. Even those who clung to circumcision did not observe the Law strictly,[81] and the relationship between Paul and Jerusalem makes open hostility completely impossible at a somewhat later time, as we shall soon see. It is true that their relations were certainly not free from tension. But the persecution of the Hellenists was not due to the 'Judaizers', but to the Jews. The 'Judaizers' certainly remained unmolested. But this means that the Jewish Christians who did not dispute the validity of the Law for Jews could live in the national community of the Jews, whilst the Jewish Christian who declared himself on principle to be free from the control of the Law was turned out of this community.[82]

Therefore, for the Jewish Christians in Palestine the question of their attitude to the Law was not only, perhaps not even principally, a theological problem, but a question of the possibility of their existence as a church in the Jewish land.

[81] Many facts support this statement: the origin of the Christian movement in Galilee ('Galilee, Galilee, thou hatest the Law, therefore thine end will be that of the robbers', *Jer. Shab.* 16; cf. W. Grundmann, *Die Geschichte Jesu Christi*, 1956, pp. 95f.; Billerbeck I, 156ff.; W. Bauer, 'Jesus der Galiläer', pp. 16ff.); the whole of the synoptic tradition (see pp. 109f.); the Easter stories which display a Christianity susceptible to ecstatic experiences, and so hardly casuistic and law-abiding; the repeated persecutions which claimed as victims, for example, the sons of Zebedee and later James, the Lord's brother. (Many sayings, too, in the synoptic tradition presuppose the state of persecution; cf. G. Strecker, *EvTh*, 1956, p. 464, who considers that the Jewish Christians' teaching about the Messiah was the motive for these persecutions. But it seems to me incredible, in view of the variety of messianic expectations in orthodox Judaism, too, that the messianic hope of the believers in Jesus—which was moreover politically harmless—could have been the cause of bloody persecution; this thesis requires at least to be substantiated thoroughly.) We must include, too, the behaviour of Peter in Antioch (see pp. 63ff.). Moreover, imminent eschatological expectation can hardly be combined with a strict legalism. There are some good comments on the problem raised here in J. Munck, *Paul*, pp. 214–17.

[82] Paul's arguments in Gal. 5.11, 6.12 are based on this state of affairs; cf. E. Hirsch in *ZNW* 29, 1930, p. 195.

II

THE 'APOSTOLIC COUNCIL'

1. WE must base our opinion of Paul's relationship to the Jewish Christians of Jerusalem on his account of the so-called 'Apostolic Council' in Gal. 2.1–10. It would only be confusing to place beside it Luke's corresponding report in Acts 15; for 'Luke's treatment of the event is only literary-theological and can make no claim to historical worth.'[1] Its historical significance lies at most in the fact that Luke presents the problem of the Law as the main issue of the conference, a fact concerning which Paul's account leaves us in no doubt either. Nevertheless the question still remains as to the meaning given to the validity of the Law in the discussion.

Paul's report serves a definite purpose. He wishes to prove in the face of the reproaches of his opponents that his gospel and his service are independent of the authority of the 'church leaders' of Jerusalem. The main substance of his concern is therefore expressed in v. 6; 'those who were of repute added nothing to me'. We certainly learn more than this from the account of the result of the conference in Jerusalem, a result which was crucial for Paul. At this conference there was, of course, in actual fact more at stake than the final statement that nothing was added to Paul. But the whole account must be read bearing in mind this central idea underlying the reason for its being reported.

Paul is not travelling as a private individual; Barnabas travels with him as a partner with equal rights. They take with them Titus, their fellow worker, as a companion. It is not suggested that they present themselves as envoys from the church of Antioch.[2] If that had been the case, it would have been significant that Antioch sent its most successful missionary team. In any case, the business in Jerusalem concerned Paul's mission, namely the mission to the Gentiles. If Paul, in v. 1f., and farther on as well,

---

[1] Dibelius, *Acts*, p. 100.
[2] Thus Haenchen, pp. 411ff./406ff.; E. Meyer, *Ursprung*, pp. 415f.

occasionally speaks in the first person singular, the reason is that he has to defend himself, not himself and Barnabas. Moreover, at the time of the Council he must certainly already have been considered as the leading partner of the pair.

Why did Paul go to Jerusalem at all? What gave rise to the conference? There were explicit negotiations resulting in definite agreements. That makes it out of the question that the intention was just to see each other, to talk together and to learn to know each other.

Paul was not summoned to Jerusalem, but came of his own freewill 'by revelation'[3] (v. 2); he tells us this himself. Therefore he obviously considers that it may have been assumed in error that he attended on the orders of the Jerusalem church. This suggests that it was the Jerusalem church in particular that was anxious for this discussion. If the need for it had lain in the circumstances of Paul's own work, even his opponents were not likely to have had the idea that the Jerusalem church had summoned him to meet them.[4] This in itself makes it unlikely that Haenchen's remark is correct: 'In fact those discussions in Jerusalem really became necessary only because the Gentile Christians in Antioch were required to accept circumcision.'[5] If that had been the case, Paul's need for a discussion would have been so urgent that Gal. 2.2a would be quite incomprehensible.

Besides, this motive can be read only into the account in Acts 15 which Haenchen, too, considers not to be authoritative, but certainly not into Gal. 2.1-10. Antioch is never mentioned in this passage; and if, in fact, envoys from Jerusalem had demanded circumcision in the Pauline mission area, they can only have been a separatist group; for according to Paul's account it was only 'false brethren secretly brought in' who created difficulties. He did not first have to obtain from those who were of repute consent for a Gentile mission free from the control of the Law. They had

[3] Paul's assurance in v. 2 that he went to Jerusalem in consequence of a revelation does not exclude the fact that the journey was a concession to constraint from outside (T. Zahn, *Galater*, p. 93).

[4] F. Sieffert, *Galater*, p. 85, follows the example of B. Weiss in thinking it even possible that the allusion to revelation is intended to exclude the view that the journey was made 'because he himself needed to go'.

[5] PP. 414/409. Similarly in R. A. Lipsius on Gal. 2.2; T. Zahn, *Galater*, pp. 93f., 106; B. Reicke, 'Der geschichtliche Hintergrund des Apostelkonzils und der Antiochia Episode', *Studia Paulina*, 1953, pp. 172ff.; E. Meyer, p. 415; F. Hahn, *Mission*, pp. 77ff.

been in sympathy with him from the beginning of his missionary activity (Gal. 1.23f.). It would have been most strange if Paul, after fifteen years of successful missionary work amongst the Gentiles, had suddenly met with opposition on matters of principle from the Jewish Christians in Jerusalem. And if *he* had then made them accept *his* way of thinking he would not have failed to report this in Gal. 2! But if, as Haenchen also assumes, the demand for circumcision emanates from a separate sectarian group, it is difficult to see why in that case Paul had come to an agreement with the 'pillars'.

H. Schlier gives another reason for Paul's journey to Jerusalem, which also finds the motive for it in *Paul's* own circumstances: 'But now there is in fact only *one* Church and only *one* gospel ... But that required an exchange of views between the new apostle extraordinary and the old regular apostles, an exchange which God forced upon him in a special revelation. The purpose of the second journey, as is explicitly said, is to bring about an agreement on the Pauline gospel.'[6] According to his further comments, Schlier holds the opinion that Paul is not satisfied with having received his gospel and apostleship from God. For the sake of the unity of the Church, the final authority of the Church, that is, the one in Jerusalem, must confirm his gospel.

These comments are not only clearly determined by Schlier's special concern; they are also in direct contradiction to what Paul says. Gal. 1 is an emphatic proof of the fact that Paul's gospel and his apostleship are completely independent of men. Gal. 2.1–10 is intended to corroborate this evidence. The 'pillars' in Jerusalem were aware of this fact when they gave their consent to the independence of the Pauline Gentile mission (Gal. 2.7ff.). The statement, 'it is said explicitly' that the purpose of the journey was to bring about an agreement on the Pauline gospel, is made by Schlier, because he translates $\dot{a}\nu\epsilon\theta\acute{\epsilon}\mu\eta\nu$ (2.2) as 'I laid before them for decision'. But $\dot{a}\nu\alpha\tau\acute{\iota}\theta\eta\mu\iota$ has at most a secondary meaning of offering for approval and denotes simply to bring before someone for consideration. This is its meaning in Gal. 2.2. It would indeed have been very late in the day if after fifteen years of intensely active preaching Paul had suddenly had to seek authorization for his

---

[6] *Galater*, p. 35. The exegesis of Sieffert, p. 91, had already pointed in this direction.

message. He emphasizes the long period of fifteen years just for the purpose of making clear the absurdity of such an interpretation of his visit by his opponents. In short, it is out of the question that the real motive for the 'Apostolic Council' was Paul's endeavour to get his gospel sanctioned by the authorities in charge.[7]

P. Althaus brings forward an argument different from, but similar to, that of H. Schlier.[8] 'The apostle to the Gentiles must have been troubled by the anxious question whether Jesus' disciples in Jerusalem would recognize his preaching.' This was not because his gospel depended on the *authority* of the Jerusalem group. But Paul knew, according to P. Althaus, that he would have toiled in vain if the connexion of his churches with the *historical disciples of the historical Jesus* had been broken. C. K. Barrett also speaks in a similar strain when writing about the 'pillar' apostles: '. . . they are the indispensable connecting links between the historical Jesus and the community of the New Age. As such they must be consulted, and fellowship with them must be maintained, at almost any cost. Upon them rested the primary responsibility of bearing witness to the resurrection.'[8a] It is only with difficulty that I can understand how this can be written at all, and particularly after expounding Gal. 1. Althaus does, however correct himself. On Gal. 2.6 he writes: 'Paul is confident about his complete authority and his message, whether the original apostles agree with it or not (1.8f.). Their judgment is a human one—What does that signify in view of the fact that Jesus Christ has appointed him?' What indeed!

These different attempts show that the question of the motive of Paul's journey to Jerusalem is harder to answer than may appear at first.[9]

---

[7] Moreover, this task would have had to be performed at latest on Paul's *first* visit to Jerusalem.

[8] Althaus, *Die kleineren Briefe des Apostel Paulus*, pp. 14f.

[8a] *Studia Paulina*, p. 18.

[9] This is evident, too, from the untenable attempt of E. Klostermann, 'Zur Apologie des Paulus Galater 1.10–2.21', *Wiss. Zeitschrift der Martin Luther Universität Halle-Wittenberg* VI/5, pp. 763–6, to find that the purpose of the journey is described in 2.4f. E. Klostermann prefers the Western text in 2.5 and paraphrases: (v. 4) '(Moreover) it was (only) on account of the false brethren brought in (in Antioch, cf. Acts 15.1f.), who slipped in to spy out our freedom that we have in Christ, that they might bring us into bondage, (v. 5) that we (leaders in Antioch) yielded submission for a moment that the truth of the gospel might be preserved for you.' The submission mentioned, if the text is understood in this sense, is then supposed to have consisted in the journey to Jerusalem!

Haenchen, Schlier and Althaus all start from the assumption that Paul begins his description of the 'Apostolic Council' by explaining the motive for his journey. They do not take into account what stimulated Paul to make this report at all. If this is done, we learn from the manner of Paul's reporting mainly only what seemed to him in the Jerusalem discussion to be particularly important as regards his *Galatian opponents at that time*, namely that in Jerusalem the independence of his gospel which was free of the Law was not called in question, but was explicitly recognized. This is why Paul declares that he went up to Jerusalem only after fourteen years of independent service (2.1). This is why he speaks of the 'revelation' (of Christ) which sent him to Jerusalem and which made it impossible to assert that he had been ordered to come by the leaders of the Jerusalem church (2.2). This is why he writes that he laid before the Jerusalem church, and indeed particularly before the δοκοῦντες there, the gospel which he preached among the Gentiles, that he had therefore brought this gospel with him to Jerusalem already, and certainly had not just received it from the people in Jerusalem (2.2). That is why he points to the success of his preaching (2.2), which he considers to be the clearest sign of the truth of his gospel, which was received independently of Jerusalem (cf. I Cor. 9.1–3; II Cor. 3.1–3, 10.12–18; Phil. 2.15f. *et passim*):[10] how can there be any success with a gospel derived from man if it had not even been possible to receive it from these men? Therefore it has not been derived from these men! That is why he emphasizes the fact that his intimate fellow worker Titus was not compelled to be circumcised, a statement which bears entirely upon the situation in Galatia and which does not even tell whether on that occasion anyone in Jerusalem demanded his circumcision.

It is obvious that in Gal. 2.1f. Paul does not intend to give an historical lecture on the reasons which led to the meeting in Jerusalem being arranged. In Gal. 2.1f. his gaze is directed entirely to the situation in Galatia. No information is provided about the motive for his journey.

Of course, his gospel was discussed—Paul leaves no doubt at all about that. Are we therefore to assume that Paul travelled to Jerusalem in order to get the *independence* of his gospel confirmed?

---

[10] Cf. Schmithals, *Apostelamt*, pp. 23ff.

But in that case there would have been need for a definite motive of which Paul gives us no hint. Besides, no one is likely to want the *independence* of his gospel to be *confirmed*. No doubt Paul thought it would be proper and desirable if a conversation with the Jerusalem group were to confirm the common nature of their service in the different ways in which it was performed: he cared a great deal for unity, particularly with the 'original church'. But the motive for his journey cannot have been a pious wish of this kind. Or had the fellowship been destroyed, and was it not repaired again until his visit to Jerusalem? Paul does not suggest anything of this kind. Must we therefore be satisfied with the information that it was because of a revelation that he travelled with Barnabas and Titus to Jerusalem?

2. Now, as we saw, it was already suggested in Gal. 2.2 that the motive for Paul's journey was to be sought not in concern for his own work, but in the problems of the Jerusalem church, and naturally in those problems connected with Paul's Gentile mission. This conjecture is corroborated when we consider the information given by Paul which is best suited to tell us about the purpose of the meeting, namely the agreements reached in Jerusalem. These were the real results and also no doubt the object which the conversations had in view.

The less important agreement, at any rate according to Paul's account, stated that Paul's churches should realize that they were pledged to remember the financial distress amongst the Jewish Christians of Judea.[11] Whatever legitimate demands of the Jerusalem church may be conjectured to lie behind this arrangement, it is in any case an unmistakable sign that the Jewish Christians and Gentile Christians wanted to hold on to the unity of the Church. They felt dependent on each other, bound to each other. But this means at the same time that in the eyes of the Jewish authorities in Jerusalem the Christian church there shared the responsibility for what happened in Paul's Christian churches.

Now, we noticed already when examining the story about Stephen that Jewish self-confidence was affected only slightly by the Christian mission to the Gentiles which disregarded the Law.[12] It was of no significance for Israel's *national* existence if Gentiles

[11] See pp. 79ff.
[12] See pp. 24f.

who disregarded the Law became Christians who did the same.[13] But the *religious* existence of the Jews was to a large extent identical with their national one, and even a purely theological judgement on the Gentile mission which rejected the Law could not stir the religious consciousness of Jews unless the Jews identified the Kingdom of Jesus with the Kingdom of God which they were awaiting. But this happened less and less in course of time, if at all.

The position was different regarding the mission to the Jews which rejected the Law. Every attempt to detach a Jew on grounds of principle from the Law was bound to arouse the unanimous resistance of Jewry, for the abolition of the Law meant the national and religious self-surrender of Judaism. A Jewry which did not observe the Law would necessarily become merged with the other nations. Whoever questioned the validity of the Law for that very reason abandoned the eschatological expectation of Israel. An attack on the Law of the Jews was an attack on Judaism as a whole. Judaism could tolerate a lax conception of the Law. It was forced to accept the apostasy of individuals; but it had to defend itself with every possible means against an antinomian propaganda.

E. Haupt[14] saw very correctly the consequences which this fact necessarily had for the original Jerusalem church: 'To abandon the forms of Judaism was equivalent to giving up peace in the primitive Church, equivalent to relinquishing any considerable success in their mission, equivalent to a war to the knife which official Judaism would have declared against it.'

This is what the Hellenists in Jerusalem had to experience. This is what James and his circle, as well as Paul[15] and his fellow workers, understood. If a Christian mission preached freedom from the Law to the Jews, then the community in Palestine was obliged for the sake of its existence to make a break with this Christianity and establish itself as an independent church. Evidence of such a breach in the community is supplied by the story of Stephen; it preserved the 'Hebrews' from the fate of the 'Hellenists'. If, therefore, the Church wished to regain and preserve its unity, it had to give up preaching freedom from the Law to the Jews: otherwise it would have prepared for the com-

---

[13] Yet see p. 25 n. 39.
[14] *Zum Verständnis des Apostolats im Neuen Testament*, p. 91.
[15] Cf. Gal. 5.11; 6.12.

munities in Judea the fate of Stephen's group. One arrangement made at the 'Apostolic Council' testifies to the desire for the Church's unity. So it is only consistent if the other and the real decision consisted of Paul's renunciation of the mission to the Jews which dissociated itself from the Law: "Ἰάκωβος καὶ Κηφᾶς καὶ Ἰωάννης, οἱ δοκοῦντες στῦλοι εἶναι, δεξιὰς ἔδωκαν ἐμοὶ καὶ Βαρναβᾷ κοινωνίας, ἵνα ἡμεῖς εἰς τὰ ἔθνη, αὐτοὶ δὲ εἰς τὴν περιτομήν' (Gal. 2.9). The working of this arrangement is unequivocal: Paul concerns himself with the Gentile mission free from the control of the Law, the mission to the Jews is the task of the Jewish Christians of Jerusalem,[16] who according to v. 8 had for some time entrusted the leadership of their mission to Peter.

This division can only be understood ethnographically.[17] τὰ ἔθνη is employed by Paul without exception in this sense and denotes the Gentiles, or Gentile Christians as contrasted with Jews, occasionally also the Gentiles as contrasted with the Christians (e.g. in I Cor. 5.1); a Jew is never included among τὰ ἔθνη.[18] In Gal. 2.9 τὰ ἔθνη is, of course, an alternative term to ἡ ἀκροβυστία, also to be understood ethnographically (Gal. 2.7; cf. Rom. 3.30; 4.9). Correspondingly ἡ περιτομή, unless the act of circumcision and the condition of being circumcised is meant, always has in Paul's writings the ethnographical sense of the Jews (Rom. 3.30; 4.9,12; 15.8; Gal. 2.12) and once the meaning of the Christians as the true people of God (Phil. 3.3). Thus the word περιτομή repeated three times in Gal. 2.7–9 is to be understood as meaning 'the Jews'.

Since this is clearly established, it is hard to understand the attempt to explain the distinction between τὰ ἔθνη and ἡ περιτομή otherwise than ethnographically. According to Schlier,[19] the terms indicate the areas in which at any time the gospel is to be

---

[16] This is the simple meaning in which Cullmann also understands the arrangement: 'The missionaries from Jerusalem were to go to the circumcised, while Paul and his fellow workers went to the Gentiles ... In opposition to the later divisions ... in spite of the complete and mutually recognized independence, they nevertheless expressed the common bond in that joint task of the collection' (*Peter*, p. 46).

[17] Thus amongst others by R. A. Lipsius, *Galater*, p. 26; A. Schweitzer, *The Mysticism of Paul the Apostle*, p. 203; Cullmann, pp. 44f.

[18] This statement takes no account of citations from the Old Testament and the Deutero-Paulines.

[19] *Galater*, p. 46; cf. F. Sieffert, *Galater*, p. 120; T. Zahn, *Galater*, p. 107; E. Haupt, *Apostolat*, p. 67; W. Foerster, 'Stephanus', p. 24; R. Liechtenhan in *Judaica* 2, pp. 57f.

preached. Unfortunately he does not go on to state on what geographical division this distinction is to be based. T. Zahn[20] appears to be thinking of Palestine on the one hand, of the rest of the world on the other.[21] But Paul's usage of τὰ ἔθνη—ἡ περιτομή is too definite to allow of the possibility that he was making a geographical division, which is also exluded by other considerations.[22]

E. Haenchen[23] rejects both interpretations and regards the formula merely as a Pauline formulation of the real result of the conference, which actually consisted in the one-sided permission for the Gentile mission free from the control of the Law, granted to Paul by the Jerusalem group. According to E. Haenchen, Paul clothes the concession in the form of a mutual agreement, in order to stand with Barnabas beside the 'pillars' as an equal in rank. This interpretation rests on the hypothesis we have already rejected, namely, that Paul travelled to Jerusalem to clear up difficulties caused to his Gentile mission by envoys from Jerusalem. Besides, it involves not a change in the shade of meaning, but a material alteration in what Paul, in fact, says.

3. The agreement made at Jerusalem consisted therefore in dividing the missionary task, so that Paul relinquished the mission to the Jews, Peter that to the Gentiles.[24]

(a) The *basis* of this arrangement is the difference in missionary methods. Paul gave up the Law: the Jerusalem group abode by

---

[20] *Galater*, pp. 106f.

[21] '... the mission field was divided in a strictly geographical sense: Palestine on one side, on the other side the world outside the Holy Land' (A. Fridrichsen, *The Apostle and his Message*, p. 12).

[22] Cf. Haenchen, pp. 413/408. H. J. Holtzmann, *Die Apostelgeschichte*, p. 103 (cf. also Sieffert, p. 120, and the earlier scholars named there), thinks that Paul understood the arrangement to be geographical, the Jerusalem group ethnographical. But it is inconceivable that it could have been so vague and therefore useless from the outset. According to Munck (p. 119) the agreement was meant to be *at the same time* geographical and ethnographical; that is something I simply cannot imagine.

[23] Pp. 414/409.

[24] E. Meyer writes in *Ursprung*, pp. 416f.: 'Barnabas and Paul were recognized as missionaries to the Gentile world. On the other hand Peter reserved the continued propagation of the gospel amongst the Jews for himself and his friends, no doubt without intending at the same time to give up the right to convert Gentiles himself. Similarly Barnabas and Paul also conversely approached Jewish congregations.' Hence in Meyer's opinion an official arrangement was made in Jerusalem which neither of the two parties was willing to respect from the start. He thinks that this is just what the 'later history' teaches (pp. 416f. n. 4). We can see what happens when the texts are read through spectacles which present a presupposed picture of history made coherent dogmatically instead of the picture being formed in accordance with the text.

it. Some commentators consider that this difference is expressed in v. 7. But τὸ εὐαγγέλιον τῆς ἀκροβυστίας or τῆς περιτομῆς surely does not mean two gospels differing in content,[25] but that the one gospel of 2.5 is preached on the one hand to the Gentiles and on the other to the Jews as separate missionary tasks, which is also the meaning of 2.8f.[26] There can, of course, be no doubt in view of 2.1ff. that the Jerusalem group, in contrast to Paul, clung to the Law. Now, Paul had just asserted (1.6–9) and emphasized with an oath that there is only one gospel and no other. Thus it is also one gospel which Paul preached subject to the exclusion of the Law, Peter subject to its inclusion. But there can be no possible doubt that to consider the Law as a means of salvation is irreconcilable with the one doctrine which both Paul and Peter proclaim. The letter to the Galatians in particular is the classic document of this gospel which is free from the Law. If the author of the letter to the Galatians is not to be considered a consummate hypocrite, the Jewish mission which Paul leaves to the Jerusalem group cannot have included the Law in the sense of its being preached by Peter as the ground of salvation. And contrariwise the Jewish Christians of Jerusalem could not recognize Paul's gospel which disregarded the Law if for them the Law had been necessary to salvation. Now, this implies that the different attitude of Paul and James to the Law cannot, at any rate primarily, have had theological reasons. There must have existed a consensus of opinion that the gospel requires the faith that 'we shall be saved through the grace of the Lord Jesus'[27] and not through the Law. Besides, this merely agrees with what we saw above (pp. 36f). If the Jewish Christians nevertheless clung to the Law, they must have done so for entirely practical reasons. We have already pictured these reasons to ourselves above: the possibility of living as a Jewish Christian church in Judea depended on recognizing at least formally the authority of the Jewish Law.

(*b*) This would also provide the explanation for the *necessity* of the division of the missionary work. Hence this division was not

---

[25] Thus, for example, A. Fridrichsen, pp. 8ff.

[26] See the commentaries on Galatians: Schlier, p. 44; Lipsius, p. 26; Sieffert, p. 116; Zahn, p. 100.

[27] Acts 15.11. There is, of course, no need to assume that the Pauline interpretation was given to this sentence by the church in Jerusalem any more than it was by the author of the Acts.

in any way based, as Meyer thought, on the 'nature of things' because 'Peter and his companions . . . could not speak Greek at all, or at the most with difficulty';[27a] it was actually quite contrary to the 'nature of things' that Paul gave up the mission amongst the Greek-speaking Jews. The necessity for this division arises rather out of the following considerations: If Paul had preached to the Jews in his world-wide mission area a gospel free from the control of the Law, and had incorporated them into his churches which disregarded the Law in their daily life, he would have made the position of the Christian churches in Judea untenable—assuming the unity of Christendom.[28] Now the Jerusalem Christians could point out that no Jews had been taken by the Christian mission out of the Law's jurisdiction. In Gal. 5.11 and 6.12 Paul provides explicit evidence that the Christian who continues to preach circumcision knows from experience that he is secure from persecution.

In theory the way of solving the dilemma might have been that every preacher should become in effect a Jew for the Jews and a Greek for the Greeks; that is to say, had preached the one gospel in such a way that none of the baptized was obliged to leave the familiar Jewish or Gentile society of his birth. But that would have been scarcely feasible in practice.

(c) In actual fact the division was arranged so that Paul for his part relinquished an organized mission to the Jews. Thus in the agreement at Jerusalem he certainly made the greater sacrifice. But he could not help making it in view of the importance to him of the original church in Jerusalem and no less of the unity of Christendom. The obvious prerequisite for what he gave up must have been the knowledge that Peter, too, preached no different gospel from his own. But Paul did not insist upon any theological considerations in the face of a non-theological understanding about the Law. On the contrary: 'Was anyone at the time of his

---

[27a] E. Meyer, p. 417.

[28] It should be recalled in this connexion that the Jews in the Diaspora were organized to some extent, especially for the payment of the Temple tax on which Jerusalem depended (H. Lietzmann, *The Beginnings of the Christian Church*, p. 77). For this financial reason alone the authorities in Jerusalem could not permit the Diaspora Jews to be alienated from the Law. Matt. 17.24–27 is sufficient evidence for the fact that the Jewish Christians paid the annual double-drachma to the Temple and did so, as it is expressly stated, for tactical reasons! Cf. R. Hummel, *Kirche und Judentum*, pp. 103ff.; G. Strecker, *Gerechtigkeit*, pp. 200f. See also p. 109 n. 18.

call already circumcised? Let him not seek to remove the marks of circumcision. Was anyone at the time of his call uncircumcised? Let him not seek circumcision. For neither circumcision counts for anything nor uncircumcision, but keeping the commandments of God. Every one should remain in the state in which he was called.' (I Cor. 7.18–20).[29] At any rate, Paul was convinced that the Jerusalem church regarded the Law to which they remained obedient as a κλῆσις in this sense. Thus the conclusion to which we had come is again confirmed, namely that the majority of Jewish Christians in Jerusalem cannot have been Judaizers strictly observing the Law.[30]

On the other hand, the Jerusalem church[31] renounced the mission amongst the Gentiles. This was an important concession, although there was hardly any dispute about it. It contained an explicit assent to Paul's gospel which rejected the Law; for the Jerusalem church relinquished all missionary work demanding

---

[29] This was also later the opinion of Justin (*Dial.* 47).

[30] Cf. G. Kittel, 'Die Stellung des Jakobus zu Judentum und Heidenchristentum', *ZNW* 30, 1931, pp. 145ff. A different view is taken by, for example, Meyer, who thinks that equality of rights of Jewish and Gentile Christians must have 'appeared to these simple people who had grown up in the strictest observance of the Law as an enormity, as a crime against God and his Law, which could not be expiated' (p. 415). Unfortunately Meyer does not tell us where he obtained such precise information about the strictly law-abiding origin of the Christians in the primitive Church.

[31] Gal. 2.7f. mentions Paul on the one hand, Peter on the other, whilst in Gal. 2.9 James, Peter, John are named on the one hand, and on the other Paul and Barnabas. This is explained by G. Klein in 'Gal. 2.6–9', pp. 282ff., by the fact that 2.7f. reflects the circumstances at the time of the 'Council', the rest of the verses those when the letter to the Galatians was written. But this is not suggested anywhere and is impossible for a variety of reasons given elsewhere (see pp. 83f. n. 13). We only need to observe here that in v. 9, which according to Klein reflects the circumstances whilst this letter was being written, Paul and Barnabas are named, although their partnership had then long ceased to exist, whilst in vv. 7f. only Paul appears, although Barnabas had travelled with Paul to Jerusalem. In fact, the whole section 2.1–10 makes it clear that the negotiations are conducted between James, Peter and John on the one hand, and Paul and Barnabas on the other. It was between these delegations that the agreement, too, was concluded; it was, in fact, an agreement of the Jewish Christians represented by Jerusalem with the Gentile Christians represented by Antioch. Therefore ἡμεῖς εἰς τὰ ἔθνη, αὐτοὶ δὲ εἰς τὴν περιτομήν means: the Jerusalemites to the Jewish Christians, the Antiochenes to the Gentile Christians; for, of course, it was not a question of a personal agreement between individual missionaries. The two delegations represented the complete and much more comprehensive activities of the two church groups.

In that case Gal. 2.7f. simply demonstrates the fact that Paul on the one hand and Peter on the other were already the prominent missionaries of their day. This has been called in question, wrongly in my opinion, with regard to Peter's missionary work by Haenchen ('Petrus-Probleme', *NTS* 7, 1960–1, pp. 192ff.). If in Gal. 2.7f. it was intended to cite an official record (see below), then for this reason alone the fact cannot be doubted.

observance of the Law amongst those who had not stood under the Law before their conversion. This concession presented no problem to the Jerusalem church. For they did not consider the Law as necessary for salvation, not even for Jews (see below). By keeping their mission within the framework of the Law (cf. Matt. 10.5f.) they were, moreover, preserved from any lapse into a freedom regarding the Law which could have been dangerous for them in Palestine.

We must not assume that the arrangements which were discussed created essentially fresh situations. They confirmed and clarified that which had long proved itself to be more or less practicable. The affair of Stephen must have conveyed a valuable lesson to primitive Christianity. It must also be recalled that Paul regarded the path of his mission to the Gentiles as having been marked out from the time of his conversion (Gal. 1.16), and that the church in Judea, from the very beginning of his missionary work, glorified God in one who preached a gospel which rejected the Law (Gal. 1.23f.). Can it be assumed that during Paul's first visit to Jerusalem (Gal. 1.18f.) the question of the relationship of the Pauline mission to the Jews and the Jewish Christians had remained unanswered or had actually not been discussed?[32] Impossible! Thus the statement 'Each of the two sides should carry on his work in accordance with the principles observed hitherto' is no doubt true for the agreement made at Jerusalem.[33]

For Peter, too, had certainly taken part in the 'Apostolic Council' as one who was already a kind of leader of the Jewish-Christian

---

[32] So Haenchen (pp. 187f. of the article just cited), since otherwise 'the serious conflict' which led fourteen years later to the 'Apostolic Council' would be inconceivable. But we saw that it was by no means 'a serious conflict' which brought Paul to Jerusalem for a second time.

[33] H. J. Holtzmann, *Die Apostelgeschichte*, p. 102. A different opinion is held by O. Cullmann, *Peter*, pp. 44ff. According to him it was decided at the 'Apostolic Council' to make a division in missionary work which had not existed before. He thinks that the churches had been mixed until that meeting. So it was tragic 'that the Jerusalem agreement did not take into account the unavoidable mixed composition of the churches' (p. 47). Hence there could not fail to arise constant interference by the Jewish Christian missionary organizations in the churches with Pauline leanings, since Jewish-Christian 'elements' had long existed in them (p. 47). Paul, on the other hand, had very properly refrained from such encroachments.

These considerations take for granted what is found, in fact, to be more and more impossible to establish, namely the existence of altercations between Paul and the Jerusalem church in his mission area. Moreover, it is to make dolts of the leaders of primitive Christianity if they are thought to be capable of concluding an agreement without ever taking its impracticability into account, because they had quite forgotten the mixed composition of their churches!

mission. In Gal. 2.7 Paul draws a parallel between himself with his missionary work amongst the Gentiles and Peter with his Jewish mission. In that case, Peter cannot have been up till then a leader in the Jerusalem church; he must, unlike James, have been occupied with a missionary task comparable with that of Paul (see p. 49 end of n. 31). This agrees with the fact that Paul when looking back on his first visit to Jerusalem already gives him the title of apostle (Gal. 1.18f.), and for Paul the prerequisite of this for its bearer is a specific missionary activity. This also provides a natural explanation why James is placed before Cephas when describing the conclusion of the agreement in Gal. 2.9f.; for at the time of the Council James occupied the leading position in the Jerusalem church, and this made him also the person who took decisions on questions of organization for the whole of Jewish Christianity. We can only imagine this precedence being given to James without difficulty and without implying any derogation of Peter if the latter was normally absent from Jerusalem. There is evidence for his absence in I Cor. 9.5, where Peter is mentioned specially alongside the apostles as one of those who are accompanied by their wives on their missionary journeys. The Ebionites, who lived in Palestine at a later date, followed James, not Peter (see also p. 104 n. 3), an indication that Peter's work and influence were not principally in Palestine, but in the Diaspora, as the first letter of Peter shows. The information given by Papias[33a] that Peter was accompanied by an interpreter might rest on an historical tradition to the extent that it assumes Peter's work to have been among the Diaspora. That Peter died at Rome is at least very probable.[33b] It is suggested by Cullmann[33c] that all the assertions made about Peter's missionary activities turn him into a missionary in the closest dependence on Jerusalem, but this is refuted by the criticism of H. Grass.[33d] This must surely be a misunderstanding of what has been asserted. For a member of the primitive Christian churches would scarcely have rated the collegiate office of the leadership of the Jerusalem church to be higher than the missionary office of the apostle. Hence at the 'Apostolic Council' the existing circumstances may, in fact, have been settled as permanently binding.

[33a] In Eusebius, *Eccl. Hist.* III, 39.15.
[33b] Cf. Cullmann, *Peter*, pp. 77ff., and the literature there cited.
[33c] *Peter*, pp. 44f.
[33d] *Ostergeschehen*, p. 97, n. 3.

But why in that case was a formal agreement required? Here the actual time of the 'Apostolic Council' is significant. It indicates that Paul was passing from his somewhat local mission in the coastal lands of the eastern Mediterranean into the world-wide mission which took him to the West. Further, Paul is leaving the area in which others have already been missionaries before and beside him and is beginning an independent mission (Rom. 15.19ff.). At this moment[34] there were good reasons for clarifying the principles underlying the points of view of both sides. This is where the real reason for the 'Council' is to be sought. Our analysis has shown clearly that its conclusions were mainly in the interests of Jerusalem. The urgency of an official agreement would be underlined if the persecution of the church in Jerusalem by the Jews, of which Acts 12 tells, might have taken place at about the time of the 'Apostolic Council'. It is a well-grounded conjecture that Paul in Gal. 2.7ff. is quoting from an official record of the outcome of the discussions drawn up in Jerusalem.[35] But in that case this record can hardly have been intended to be used within the church, but to serve as documentary evidence for the Jewish authorities, who were possibly represented by observers at the conference (see pp. 107f.). In any case the agreements protected the Jerusalem church from persecution by the Jewish authorities so far as this could be done whilst the Gentile mission continued; of course, these agreements also created clear conditions for the churches about to be formed in the Diaspora.

A further consideration must be added. We have already said that the 'Apostolic Council' indicated the beginning of Paul's independent missionary work. This work was carried on at first with Barnabas as an intimate fellow worker. Acts gives an account of it in chs. 13f. in the form of a description of the so-called first missionary journey. After the unfortunate incident at Antioch, Silvanus, and later Timothy, replaced Barnabas; now their mission

---

[34] It takes place presumably before the events described by Luke as the first missionary journey (Acts 13f.) (see Haenchen, pp. 386/380). Another view is held by Kümmel in *TR* 17, 1948, pp. 30ff. (see his references); but the Council followed immediately upon Paul's work in Syria and Cilicia (cf. Gal. 1.21–2.1).

[35] Cf., e.g., Cullmann, *Peter*, p. 20, and in *TWNT* VI, p. 100, n. 6; E. Dinkler in *VF*, 1953–5, pp. 182f.; Klein, 'Gal. 2.6–9', pp. 283f. Dinkler proposes as a possible reconstruction of the passage from the source quoted by Paul: . . . ὅτι Παῦλος πιστεύει τὸ εὐαγγέλιον τῆς ἀκροβυστίας καθὼς Πέτρος τῆς περιτομῆς, ὁ γὰρ ἐνεργήσας Πέτρῳ εἰς ἀποστολὴν τῆς περιτομῆς ἐνήργησεν καὶ Παύλῳ εἰς τὰ ἔθνη . . .

takes them into western Asia Minor and Greece. In all these areas there was not yet an organized Christian mission. It is Paul who founds the first churches. They are Gentile-Christian churches, the early members of which are presumably mainly drawn from among the σεβόμενοι (see below).

In the cities in which Paul preached to the Gentiles there were also Jewish minorities of varying size. Paul was prevented by his consideration for his brethren in Christ at Jerusalem from preaching to these Jews, too, his gospel which disclaimed the Law and incorporating them into his churches which lived in freedom from the Law. On the other hand, he was not indifferent to the fate of his 'brothers according to the flesh'. Far from it; Rom. 9–11 bears eloquent witness to his deeply rooted, heartfelt zeal for his nation: 'I am speaking the truth in Christ, I am not lying; my conscience bears me witness in the Holy Spirit, that I have great sorrow and unceasing anguish in my heart. For I could wish that I myself were accursed and cut off from Christ for the sake of my brethren, my kinsmen by race. They are Israelites, and to them belong the sonship, the glory, the covenants, the giving of the law, the worship and the promises; to them belong the patriarchs, and of their race, according to the flesh, is the Christ . . .' (Rom. 9. 1–5).

The attitude of the apostle towards his nation and the God of his fathers, which prompts these words, makes it seem inconceivable that Paul could have preached to the Gentiles and established churches from amongst them without inquiring about the Jews who lived in the same place or area. A mission to the Gentiles without another at the same time to the Jews could hardly be imagined by Paul. He must therefore have received an assurance from the outset that a Jewish mission would be organized and carried on parallel with his Gentile mission.

Although he could not preach to the Jews his gospel free from the Law, yet he saw in his preaching to the Gentiles a real piece of service for his 'kinsmen by race': 'Inasmuch as I am an apostle to the Gentiles, I magnify my ministry in order to make my fellow Jews jealous, and thus save some of them' (Rom. 11.13f.). But such an expectation presupposes that the gospel is being preached to the Jews as well and that they are being gathered into churches of their own observance.

This means that before Paul began his independent missionary work in regions where no one had preached hitherto he had to satisfy himself that a Jewish-Christian mission would take its place beside the Gentile-Christian mission. It is just this which happened at the 'Apostolic Council'. We have already established the fact that the agreements reached there did not create any essentially fresh conditions. Consequently the agreement may have been fixed explicitly and possibly recorded in an official document or even as a compact in view of the *new* mission area which was now proposed. Arrangements are made for the new area which is about to be opened up, 'that we should go to the Gentiles and they to the circumcised' (Gal. 2.9b). Thus the agreement laid upon the Jewish Christians of Jerusalem the obligation to carry the gospel to the Jews in those places in which Paul preached to the Gentiles; and for Paul this aspect of the agreement may have had a significance which was not to be underrated. The reason why Paul, at a later date before his journey to Spain, once more takes the dangerous road to Jerusalem may be in large part his desire to discuss and make sure that the Jerusalem agreement would be carried out in the western Mediterranean as well. It was not by chance that Peter and Paul were in Rome together!

All that has been said by no means prevents us from recognizing that the arrangement made in Jerusalem was in the interests of the *Jewish Christians*. Paul wanted to secure by an arrangement with Jerusalem a guarantee for a mission which he had at heart amongst the Jews in his mission area, and his reason for doing so was just this, that in the interests of the Jerusalem Christians he had to refrain from having a mission of his own amongst the Jews.

4. Now, there are weighty objections to this description of what happened. It is just these objections which the commentators think they must urge against an ethnographical understanding of the agreement reported by Paul, in spite of the wording which clearly points to it. E. Haenchen deals with this understanding by an implied glance at the account of Paul's missionary activity in Acts, and with the remark that an agreement of this kind would have forbidden Paul to make any contact with the synagogues.[36] This objection will have to be expanded into the basic question: Did Paul really relinquish the mission to the Jews?

When Paul was writing Gal. 2 the Jerusalem agreement must

[36] Pp. 414/409.

still have been in force. Since the letter to the Galatians was probably written during Paul's so-called third missionary journey, that arrangement must have been binding on the apostle at least during his most important missionary period. Did Paul not preach to the Jews during this time?

It must be noticed that the problem cannot be solved by pointing to the greater or smaller number of Jews by birth in Paul's Churches. Paul neither desired, nor was able nor needed to raise objections if Jews joined one of his churches and thereby gave up observing the Law—as he had done. According to careful estimates, more than five million Jews lived in the Roman Empire. Not all of them were devout Jews. To observe the Law in the midst of a pagan environment involved social restrictions. Not all accepted these and the synagogue had no power to retain its disloyal members. It is unlikely that many apostates from Judaism became 'believing' Gentiles. The man who left the congregation of the synagogue lived in 'no-man's-land'.[37] Naturally a lost sheep of this kind easily found his way into a Gentile-Christian church which combined the heritage of his fathers with freedom from the Law. These men had long since been lost to the synagogue. Paul was not responsible for their giving up the Law. No less a person than Timothy, the uncircumcised offspring of a Jewish-Gentile mixed marriage, is an example of this group (Acts 16.1). When individual members of the synagogue voluntarily joined the church it was unjust to accuse Paul of carrying on propaganda to persuade Jews to abandon the Law (Acts 18.8; the conversion of Crispus evidently remained fixed as a special case in the memory of the church; cf. I Cor. 1.14).

It certainly seems as though hardly any Jews belonged to Paul's churches. It is agreed today that the letters to Corinth, Galatia, Philippi and Thessalonica are addressed to *Gentile*-Christian churches. I Thess. 1.9 (cf. I Cor. 12.2; Gal. 4.8) applies to the churches of the third missionary journey as a whole:'... how you turned to God from idols, to serve a living and true God'. Paul calls the churches definitely 'churches of the Gentiles' (Rom. 16.4);[38] he even addresses the members of the church directly as

[37] Cf. W. Foerster, *Zeitgeschichte* II, pp. 254f.
[38] This name presupposes the other one, namely 'churches of the Jews'. Clearly these are the technical names for the churches which were to be organized separately in accordance with the agreement at the 'Apostolic Council'.

'you Gentiles' (Rom. 11.13). Only exceptionally and individually can Jews have been represented amongst them.[39]

Furthermore, Paul always designates himself with emphasis as the apostle to the Gentiles[40] (Rom. 11.13; 15.16, 18; Gal. 2.2; I Thess. 2.16). That is the name by which he lives on in the conciousness of Christendom: Eph. 3.1, 8; I Tim. 2.7. Already at his conversion God appointed him to be a missionary to the Gentiles: Gal. 1.16.[41] The passages cited allow of no doubt that Paul is not carrying on, *alongside* a mission to the Jews, a mission to the Gentiles as well,[42] but that he was a missionary to the Gentiles, unlike the others who were missionaries to the Jews. It is just this that we are told in Gal. 2.9, too.

In Rom. 9-11 Paul speaks at length about the expected conversion of the Jews. He could wish himself to be accursed if only his 'brothers according to the flesh' might find their way to Christ (9.1ff.). That Israel may be saved is his heart's desire and earnest prayer (10.1). For this purpose preaching is necessary (10.12ff.). But in what does Paul's contribution for saving the Jews consist? It is in the mission to the Gentiles! In the face of Israel's blindness Paul explicitly extols his apostolate to the Gentiles because their salvation might perhaps make Israel jealous and willing to imitate them (11.11ff.).

All this is so clear that it is hard to imagine how modern theologians can assume as a matter of course that Paul naturally preached to the Jews as well as to the Gentiles. Haupt does indeed take pains to prove 'that Paul did not renounce activity amongst the Jews'.[43] He rests his proof on I Cor. 9.20 alone: 'To the Jews I became as a Jew, in order to win Jews; to those under the law

---

[39] For additional material on this from Paul's letters see Munck, *Paul*, pp. 200ff.

[40] Cf. Munck, p. 41: W. Grundmann, 'Paulus, aus dem Volke Israel, Apostel der Völker', *Novum Testamentum*, 4, 1960, pp. 267ff.

[41] This is an undoubtedly correct statement. For Paul had persecuted the Christians because they denied the Jewish community's exclusive claim to salvation, which was based on the Law. His conversion was a conversion to the Christian gospel's message of universal salvation. Paul can scarcely have emphasized that he is an apostle to the Gentiles only after the agreement of Jerusalem: on the contrary, what he emphasizes is the accepted basis of this agreement (cf. Gal. 2.7f.).

[42] There are no grounds for E. Haupt's opinion (in *Apostolat*, p. 66) that the passages cited only state that *in fact* Paul's vocation became limited more and more to the Gentile world and that he looked upon that as his *special* sphere. The same is true of W. Michaelis's assertion that Paul, too, preached circumcision at first ('Judaistische Heidenchristen', *ZNW* 30, 1931, p. 88).

[43] *Apostolat*, p. 65; cf. E. Preuschen, *Die Apostelgeschichte*, p. 86; especially R. Liechtenhan in *Judaica* 2, pp. 56ff.

I became as one under the law—though not being myself under the law—that I might win those under the law.' But this passage cannot bear the burden of proof placed upon it. If it were to serve the purpose required by Haupt, it would assume that Paul had preached the gospel without the Law to the Gentiles and with the Law to the Jews, as occasion demanded. But that would have been an impossible mode of propaganda, especially as in practice it would have had to result in a separate organization for each church. Instead we must follow Lietzmann[44] in placing I Cor. 9.20 beside passages such as Acts 16.3; 18.18; 21.20–26 as regards their subject-matter, passages which need to be examined critically, a task which we are reserving for later (see pp. 85ff.). Yet there is no doubt that Paul could keep the requirements of the Law, if thereby he was enabled to clear an obstacle out of the path of the gospel, irrespective of the fact whether it was he or the Jerusalem church or others who faced these obstacles; this by no means proves that Paul preached amongst the Jews nor is it even said that he did. For Paul's preaching to the Jews H. Schlier refers also to Rom. 11.13f.;[45] I cannot follow this argument.[46]

Only the accounts in the Acts would remain; in these Paul is described as a frustrated missionary to the Jews, who preaches to the Gentiles only because the Jews reject him.[46a] Even at his call he was sent both to the Gentiles and to the Jews.[46b] It is generally agreed that behind the stereotyped accounts in the Acts, which regard Paul as constantly making contact with the synagogues and being driven thence to the Gentiles, a Lucan bias is to be sought.[47]

In my opinion the real object of this bias has not yet been sufficiently explained. It is Haenchen who has concerned himself particularly with this whole problem and has defined Luke's bias more precisely as being *apologetic*. In the prolonged apologetic discussion which Luke holds in the Acts with the Roman Govern-

---

[44] *Korinther*, p. 43.
[45] *Galater*, p. 46, n. 2.
[46] A. Fridrichsen's reference to Rom. 1.13f. (*The Apostle and his Message*, p. 12) is still more unsuccessful. Here Paul seems to be excluding the Jews in particular from those to whom he is 'under an obligation' as an apostle.
[46a] Acts 13.5, 14, 42ff.; 14.1ff.; 17.1ff., 10; 18.4ff., 19 (26); 19.8f.; 22.17ff.; 28.17–28.
[46b] Acts 9.15; 22.15; 26.19ff.
[47] Cf. Dibelius, *Acts*, pp. 149f.

ment, Luke's particular object, amongst others, is to declare Christianity to be a Jewish αἱρεσις and therefore a *religio licita*.[48] This object is promoted by the numerous features of Luke's descriptions in which the intimate connexion of the Christian fellowship with the Jewish religion is set out.[49] Conzelmann[50] is right in refuting this. He regards Luke's presentation as confined to the church and as due to his interest in salvation history. That is right, but insufficient; for it must still be asked how he came to have this interest. The fact that the parousia was delayed did not in itself supply the reason for this particular interest, which amongst other things makes Paul a Pharisee.

W. Eltester[51] answers this question by explaining that in Luke's time Gentile Christianity began to feel doubtful whether it had the right to use the Old Testament, the book of the Jews, as a charter of its own faith. The Lucan scheme answers this question in the affirmative. This, too, is both correct[52] and insufficient, for we must now ask who caused the Church to have any doubts about an appeal to the Old Testament which at the outset had been taken for granted. Is there anyone before Marcion who did this?

Haenchen[53] does indeed reject Eltester's interpretation, but now gives an explanation other than his former one of Luke's presentation of Paul as a devout Jew who upheld the Law. He thinks that Luke was wrestling with the problem how the Jews, who were in his day already 'written off' by the Church, could have thrown away the salvation promised to them. He replies that 'it was not the fault of early Christianity if the Jews rejected the salvation offered to them'; for the first Christians, including Paul, lived as devout Jews. But we must ask Haenchen whether in Luke's lifetime anyone had reproached the Christians who had long since 'written off' the Jews for the Jews' loss of salvation, and had done so to such an extent that Luke was obliged to write an apology which grotesquely distorted the actual circumstances. Of course, no one

---

[48] Haenchen, pp. 565/560; H. J. Holtzmann, *Die Apostelgeschichte*, p. 17; G. P. Wetter, *ARW* 21, p. 414.
[49] See in Haenchen, pp. 186/182; 178/174; 283/276; 482/476; 565/560; 571f./566; 575/570ff.; 624ff./619ff.; 663ff./654ff; cf. G. Klein, 'Besprechung', pp. 369f.
[50] In his review of Haenchen's commentary, *TLZ* 85, 1960, cols. 244f.
[51] 'Lukas und Paulus', in *Eranion, Festschrift für H. Hommel*, 1961, pp. 1–17.
[52] I differ from Eltester in considering it completely impossible that it was Paul's companion, Luke, who in his own times drew such a completely distorted picture of his apostolic teacher in order to satisfy the requirements we have mentioned.
[53] 13th ed., pp. 680f.

had done so! And the Jews' lack of faith cannot have distressed Luke as a real theological problem; for this problem is not solved by pointing to the Christians' innocence (a different view is expressed in Rom. 9–11). Finally, Luke by his solution would, at the worst, have created a greater problem than the one he had solved could have been; for then the question arises concerning the right of the church amongst the Gentiles to abandon its Jewish foundations in post-Pauline times.

It is evident that Luke's particular purpose in presenting Christianity as the true Judaism has not yet been sufficiently explained. But of the purpose itself there can be no doubt. The Gentile mission presented Luke in that case with a special problem. According to Luke it was due on the one hand to God's explicit commission, although the church and the missionaries opposed it (Acts 10f.; 15.7–21; 22.17ff.). On the other hand, it is entirely the fault of the Jews that the Christians had to organize themselves apart from the synagogues (cf. Acts 13.42ff. and the other passages just cited). 'It is not the fault of the Christians and of Christianity that it became a religion distinct from Judaism and subject to persecution alongside it.'[54]

Therefore the object of Luke's literary efforts provides ample grounds for his attempt to represent Paul as a frustrated missionary to the Jews. Admittedly 'it ought not to have been questioned that Paul in fact visited the existing synagogues in order to make contact with the σεβόμενοι.'[55] 'The fact that Paul is never allowed to turn to the Gentiles until he is rejected by the Jews produces a false theory out of his natural attempts to establish a relationship with the synagogue.'[56] These sentences reproduce the settled opinion prevailing today, whether it is based on an historical core in Luke's presentation or with Haenchen on the general consideration that Paul, for reasons of practical convenience, 'naturally' in each case started his mission in the synagogue. But neither the alleged historical core of Luke's tendentious account, nor general considerations about the most practical method of Paul's missionary work, can stand up against the unequivocal meaning of what Paul himself says. In spite of Acts Paul did not engage in a

---

[54] Haenchen, pp. 482/478.
[55] Haenchen, pp. 450/445.
[56] Haenchen, pp. 362/356. Cf. H. Grass, *Ostergeschehen*, p. 214, n. 1.

mission to the Jews, however, inconvenient that may have been thought to be.

It could scarcely be said in any case that it was convenient for Paul to make contact with the synagogues. The core of his message was that Christ is the goal of the Law. Nowhere would he expect to meet greater resistance to his preaching, nowhere must this resistance be more intense and violent than in the synagogue. If Paul had, in fact, started his preaching by making contact with the synagogue, this course of action would have implied the conscious intention of provoking the most severe opposition right at the beginning of his preaching, of endangering any success from the start and at least of making it *appear* that the mission to the Gentiles—as described by Luke—was the enforced result of Jewish opposition to the message about Christ. All this could not be what the apostle intended, nor could Paul be believed to be capable of concealing at first the real content of his message concerning Christ in order to let the cat out of the bag only after he had established the needful personal authority. Besides, such an attempt would scarcely have been successful; for if he was really travelling from synagogue to synagogue, he could hardly visit a fresh synagogue as a quite unknown person; his reputation preceded him. To sum up: it is almost impossible to imagine Paul beginning his preaching in the synagogues.

A quite incomprehensible opinion is expressed by E. Meyer,[56a] namely that Barnabas and Paul *in spite* of the explicit prohibition of this practice by the Apostolic Council turned to the Jewish communities as well; for 'there was in fact no other way in which they could approach the Gentiles when they began operations in a fresh place.'

In saying this we are not denying but asserting that Paul, when starting a mission, endeavoured to establish a connexion with 'God-fearers' in each place.[57] These people are not members of the Jewish community and subject to the Law, but uncircumcised Gentiles, who were not reckoned by the Jews as belonging to them, but on the contrary were later definitely cast out.[58] In Acts 16.11-15 some information, possibly from a travel diary

---

[56a] *Ursprung*, p. 417.
[57] Cf. the good examination of our problem in Holtzmann, pp. 13ff.
[58] W. Foerster, *Zeitgeschichte* II, p. 233f.; K. G. Kuhn in *TWNT* VI, pp. 743f.

based on an eyewitness report, is reproduced. It describes Paul on his arrival in Philippi as being on the look-out for such σεβόμενοι. In contrast to the typically Lucan account there is no mention either of Jews or of a synagogue. In Corinth, too, Paul preached with success in the house of a 'God-fearer' named Titius Justus; Crispus, the ruler of the synagogue, was baptized there (Acts 18.7f.). These statements give the impression of being reliable and perhaps come from a source which told how Paul first followed his trade at the house of Aquila and Priscilla (18.1–3), but on the arrival of Silas and Timothy began to undertake mission-work energetically (18.5a) and did so, in fact, in the house of Titius Justus (18.7f.). The intervening notes about Paul's preaching in the synagogue do not at any point make the impression that they had been found ready to hand by Luke; on the contrary they reveal all through a typically Lucan stamp and may go back completely to Luke himself.[59] The source worked up by him knew nothing about Paul preaching in the synagogue; it related merely how Paul gets in touch with the σεβόμενοι.

Presumably Paul's first churches consisted chiefly of such 'God-fearers'.[60] Unfortunately we know but very little about the extent of proselytism in the period before AD 70, since after 70 Jewry cut itself off from the Gentiles. But H. J. Schoeps[61] has persuaded me that we can hardly overestimate the success of the Jewish propaganda amongst the Gentiles before 70, that this propaganda had reached its zenith in Paul's time, and that its fruits fell into the lap of early Christianity. In any case there was no occasion for Paul to start his missionary work with the Jews, even for reasons of expediency. The Gentile 'God-fearers' were much more sympathetic and suitable listeners for his gospel, which dispensed with the Law. Schoeps is right in considering that 'Rom. 9–11 can best be understood as an exhortation to Gentile Christians who had already passed through the Jewish mission, thus had already belonged to the σεβόμενοι'.[61a] In that

---

[59] It is probably more than doubtful that a metropolis like Corinth possessed only one synagogue, as Luke assumes here.

[60] So also A. von Harnack, *Marcion*, p. 22.

[61] *Paulus*, pp. 233ff. See the further references there. Cf. also P. Dalbert, *Missionsliteratur*, pp. 21ff.; J. Leipoldt, *Taufe*, pp. 4ff.; E. Lerle, *Proselytenwerbung und Urchristentum*, 1960, pp. 9ff.; W. G. Braude, *Jewish Proselyting in the First Five Centuries of the Common Era*, 1940.

[61a] *Paulus*, p. 249.

case the church in Rome, which was not founded by Paul, also consisted essentially of former 'God-fearers'. This is supported by the natural manner in which Paul in his letters assumes the Old Testament to be familiar and well known to his churches.

Finally, we must point to the fact that we can still glean in several places from the scanty information which has been preserved the division between the churches of Paul and of Peter,[62] positively, in fact, in Corinth (I Cor. 1.12) and Antioch, possibly also in Ephesus and Rome.[63] In the small places with insignificant Jewish communities, independent Jewish Christian churches are anyhow not to be expected.

The form of address in I Peter does not explicitly presuppose the actual independence of Jewish-Christian churches; but it shows that at the end of the first century Peter was regarded as *the* missionary to the Jews in the Diaspora, a correct view found also in Eusebius.[63a] It cannot be seriously denied that Peter was at work in the Diaspora as a missionary to the Jews, and it is true to say of his activities '. . . he was never in competition with Paul.'[64]

---

[62] E. Hirsch ('Petrus und Paulus', *ZNW* 29, 1930, p. 73) considers that '. . . the way in which both Jerusalem and Paul viewed the oneness of the Church excludes the existence of two churches side by side in one place.' This is a complete contradiction of the agreement at the 'Apostolic Council' and is moreover unfounded.

[63] See Schmithals, *Die Gnosis in Korinth*, p. 167 n. 1; and 'Die Irrlehrer von Röm. 16.17–20', *Studia Theologica* 13, 1959, p. 53; Cullmann, *Peter*, pp. 54ff.

[63a] *Eccl. Hist.* III, 4.1ff.

[64] M. Dibelius, *Botschaft und Geschichte* II, p. 202. Cf. also H. Lietzmann, 'Die Reisen des Petrus', in *Kleine Schriften* II, pp. 287ff.

III

THE UNFORTUNATE INCIDENT IN ANTIOCH

1. THE conception we have formed so far of the relationship between Paul and James must hold good for Paul's account of his controversy with Peter in Antioch which follows his description of the 'Apostolic Council' (Gal. 2.11ff.).

Paul does not indicate any date for his clash with Peter. There should certainly be no doubt, in view of the chronological sequence set out in the account from 1.13 onwards, that this unpleasant occurrence happened after the 'Apostolic Council'. Only exceedingly weighty reasons could induce us to reverse the order of Paul's report. No such reasons appear.[1] On the other hand, the clash in Antioch need not have followed *immediately* on the 'Apostolic Council'. If the conference in Jerusalem occurred *before* the missionary activity recorded in Acts 13f., as seems probable,[2] then Paul had the disagreement with Peter *after* this missionary journey; for it is certain that this clash brought to an end the working partnership between Paul and Barnabas (see below) which still existed throughout the first missionary journey. We can indeed establish nothing more definite about it.

In the section now to be examined we must pay even more attention than in the case of Gal. 2.1–10 to Paul's purpose in writing this account. He wants to demonstrate his independence from the pillars in Jerusalem, and here from Peter. The incident itself naturally arose out of other causes and it did not primarily result in proving Paul's independence. But we learn about what *actually* happened in Antioch only as part of a very tendentious report.

In Antioch Paul was obliged to stand up to Peter, who was at

---

[1] Cf. J. Dupont, 'Pierre et Paul à Antioche et à Jérusalem', *Recherches de Science religieuse* 45, 1957, pp. 42–60; 225–39, who examines and criticizes the attempts of T. Zahn, J. Munck and H. M. Féret to reverse the order of the events.
[2] Haenchen, pp. 386f./380f.

work there, because the latter was condemning himself by his own behaviour (Gal. 2.11). What had happened? At first Peter regularly sat at table with the Gentile Christians. This was no serious offence against the Law. The Old Testament contains no regulation forbidding a Jew to have table-fellowship with Gentiles. Rules of this kind came into use later. It is uncertain whether, and to what extent, the scribes' instructions in this sense were already developed in New Testament times; but the author of Acts, who certainly did not write before the second century, regarded it as settled that Jews and Gentiles are not allowed to eat together: Acts 10.28; 11.3; cf. John 18.28; Luke 15.2; Mark 7.1ff.; Justin, *Dial.* 47. However, numerous statements in rabbinic literature show that, in fact, table-fellowship was conceded not infrequently and with certain reservations. Pious Jews may also have brought their own food with them to the table of a Gentile host.[3] In view of these facts the liberty which Peter took in Antioch for the sake of fellowship in the church need not necessarily denote a radical breach of the Law. Table-fellowship with the Gentiles therefore hardly meant for Peter, and even less for Paul, a conscious repudiation of the Jerusalem agreement which required Peter, as a missionary to the Jews, to observe the Law to a certain extent. Yet this confirms what we have realized so far, namely that Peter and the Jerusalem church were not zealous upholders of the Law.

But the use which Peter made of the freedom possible to him presumably *within* Jewish Christianity has yet another aspect. Schweitzer writes: 'That the question at Antioch concerned eating together at the Lord's Supper is so obvious that Paul does not think it necessary to say so expressly.'[4] This opinion seems to me somewhat too definite in view of the general phrase: μετὰ τῶν ἐθνῶν συνήσθιεν. But there is well-founded agreement amongst commentators that the common meal received its importance from the celebration of the cultic meal in particular.[5] Basically the celebration of meals in common meant that the separation between the Jewish-Christian and the Gentile-Christian churches was abolished. It must be well understood that Peter's behaviour does not at all presuppose that in general he had freed himself,

[3] On all this see Billerbeck III, pp. 421f.; IV, pp. 374ff.; A. Schweitzer, *Mysticism*, pp. 196f.
[4] P. 196.
[5] It is true that Paul does not indicate that he is thinking especially of cultic meals.

and still less Jewish Christians, from the Law altogether, and certainly not from a Jewish mission which dispensed with the Law; in this respect the arrangements made in Jerusalem will not have been violated in Antioch either. But the visible distinction between the different church groups was obliterated by the common meal, even if in other matters the Jewish Christians lived according to the Law.[6] Peter's behaviour did not conflict completely with the wording of the Jerusalem agreement, but it ran counter to its intention.

That must have stimulated the church in Jerusalem to take action. Table-fellowship with Gentile Christians was a first step on a road on which there was no stopping, and, in the eyes of the Jews standing outside, this step for uniting the groups in the community must have made it look as if Jewish Christianity had already abandoned the Law completely. That it was none other than Peter, head of the mission to the Jews which observed the Law, who was taking part in these happenings, and that they took place in the influential metropolis of Antioch, must have seemed particularly serious to the Jerusalem church. We do not know whether they had already experienced difficulties from the Jews on account of the behaviour of Jewish Christians in Antioch, or whether they merely feared them. In either case they feel obliged to check the development which had been set going there. Thus one day τινὰς ἀπὸ 'Ιακώβου make their appearance in Antioch. Their remonstrances do not fail to make an impression on Peter. He withdraws from the Gentile Christians and 'separates himself' (Gal. 2.12). The rest of the Jewish Christians follow his example (Gal. 2.13); even Barnabas remembers his Jewish origin and joins this group which thereby returns to the undiminished independence of its existence as a church.

[6] We see here what problems were raised by the necessary arrangement in Jerusalem when and because Christians knew that they were one Church. In the long run—which in primitive Christianity was not, of course, taken into account—it was not practicable for them to live side by side in two groups. This state of affairs therefore did not last long; fortunately it did not need to last long. With the destruction of Jerusalem in 70 the Jews lost the possibility of dictating to the Christians in Palestine how they should live. There was no longer any necessity to separate the Jewish-Christian churches from the Gentile Christians in the Roman Empire. The fight against Gnosis may have provided a final fillip to bring the two groups together. So it is not surprising that from as early as the second century we have no reliable information—apart from Palestine and the sects—concerning independent metropolitan churches observing Jewish-Christian rules. See also below, pp. 114ff.

2. Paul states explicitly that Peter took his fateful step from fear of the party ἐκ περιτομῆς (2.12). If he made his decision from fear of men, then at all events it was not owing to theological opinions. It was not for the sake of a better righteousness that Peter again upheld a separate Jewish Christian life, but from some kind of practical considerations. Of whom was he afraid?

The commentators take it for granted that those ἐκ περιτομῆς means Jewish Christians; in fact, those who turned up in Antioch or those who sent them from Jerusalem, the church in Jerusalem under the leadership of James. This meaning seems so obvious[7] that the possibility of Peter having acted as he did from fear of the *Jews* is usually never contemplated. And yet in my opinion this is the only right answer.

It is surely impossible that Peter could be afraid of the party of James. What could they have done to him and to the church? It is absurd to assume that the primitive church in Jerusalem which had worries enough about its own bare existence could have possessed any means of enforcing its authority against the Antiochene Christians. It could not even do so with regard to its own members. Or is Peter thought to have feared the moral anathema of Jerusalem? But the Jewish Christians of Antioch were on his side, as 2.13 shows.

Moreover, how might he ever have had anything to fear from James? The laxity shown by Peter in his understanding of the Law could arouse the dangerous wrath only of legalist Judaizers. We have seen that the body of Christians in Jerusalem, at any rate as a whole, was not a community full of zeal for the Law.[8] And if it had been zealous, what was right and reasonable as regards fellowship with the Jerusalem party for Paul, who disregarded the Law, would be just as right and reasonable for a Peter who disregarded the Law.

[7] '. . . . it becomes almost inescapable to see in οἱ ἐκ περιτομῆς men from Jerusalem, and in that case naturally the party of James' (G. Klein, 'Verleugnung', p. 321, n. 4). But why 'naturally'?

[8] T. Zahn, *Galater*, pp. 114f., therefore explains ἐλθεῖν τινας ἀπὸ 'Ιακώβου to mean that the messengers were not sent by James, but had unlawfully claimed his authority. Impossible!

Presumably similar considerations underlie Kümmel's opinion (*RGG*³ VI, col. 1189) that an out-and-out conservative minority in the Jerusalem church had opposed the settlement of the 'Apostolic Council' agreed between James and Paul. But firstly Paul says explicitly that the envoys had come from *James*, and secondly they are, in fact, insisting, in Peter's case, just on the *observance* of the Jerusalem arrangement.

Further, it seems improbable from the point of view of language also that in the sentence: ὅτε δὲ ἦλθον, ὑπέστελλεν καὶ ἀφώριζεν ἑαυτόν, φοβούμενος τοὺς ἐκ περιτομῆς (2.12) the subject of ἦλθον and the object of φοβούμενος are thought to be the same: if that was the meaning, a simple αὐτούς which could not be misunderstood would be expected instead of τοὺς ἐκ περιτομῆς.

Finally, Paul *always* uses ἐκ περιτομῆς to denote the Jew by birth as such, contrasted with the Gentile, never the Jewish Christian contrasted with the Gentile Christian. The phrase had just been used in this way (2.7ff.).[9] Hence ἐκ περιτομῆς can less than ever mean a name for the strictly law-abiding Jewish Christians in particular. But this specific meaning would have had to be given to Gal. 2.12 in the traditional exegesis, since actually Peter, too, together with the Antiochene Jewish-Christian community, belongs to the Jewish Christians in general. Peter cannot after all be afraid of himself!

To sum up the argument: It was fear of the Jews which determined Peter's decision.[10] Probably it was less a question of fear regarding the Antiochene church, although the Jewish community in Antioch, like that in Alexandria, were under an archon who was not likely to be without means of enforcing his authority.[11] But it was undoubtedly his fears for the churches of Judea; in fact, just those fears which brought James's messengers to Antioch.[12] After all, we must remember that the altercation in

[9] Cf. G. Dix, *Jew and Greek*, 1953, pp. 42f.
[10] So also B. Reicke in *Studia Paulina*, pp. 176ff., as I have seen since writing the above. B. Reicke is correct in speaking of the terrible pressure under which Christianity in Jerusalem was living, and declares this to be the cause of the 'Judaistic' bias expressed in the deputation of James to Peter. But he does not see that, in fact, this pressure already underlay the agreement of the 'Apostolic Council', and thinks that he must presuppose a strong Judaistic declension of the Jewish Christians from that Council to the incident in Antioch. This is unnecessary and unfounded, even if Reicke may be right when he remarks that the pressure of the Jews on the Jewish Christians became progressively stronger. Dix, too (pp. 42ff.), understands οἱ ἐκ περιτομῆς to be the Jews.

Munck, *Paul*, pp. 106ff., also states the meaning of οἱ ἐκ περιτομῆς to be the Jews, and is evidently the first to do so. In view of the frequent quite erroneous theories and exegeses in his book, one hesitates to refer to it. Yet his reflections on this matter and some other comments are very far-seeing, even though he gives a completely wrong explanation of the 'fear of the Jews'. The objections of K. Wegenast, *Das Verständnis der Tradition bei Paulus*, p. 48 n. 2, to Munch's theory in my opinion only reveal the straits of whoever wishes to defend the interpretation of the disputed passage as referring to the Jewish Christians in Jerusalem.

[11] Jos. *Bell.* VII, 3.3.
[12] Thus Dix, pp. 43ff., is essentially correct: 'What the messengers "from James" brought to Peter was not an ultimatum from a suddenly overwhelming Jewish-

Antioch took place in the period between the violent death of James, the son of Zebedee (Acts 12.2), and the martyrdom of James, the brother of the Lord! Peter himself seemed only shortly before to have barely escaped a martyr's death (Acts 12). In view of this the honourable nature and conscientiousness of his decision must not be called in question.

If this is the position, then it does not surprise us that Paul utters no word of criticism against either James's messengers or James himself.[13] He could not regard as unjustified their demand that the Jewish-Christian church should keep itself separate, especially as this agreed with the sense of the Jerusalem arrangement. 'Neither the envoys from James nor Peter nor Barnabas became disloyal to the agreement of Jerusalem.'[14] Certainly not! It was not the wishes of the primitive church in Jerusalem but the personal behaviour of Peter[15] which provoked anger and criticism in Paul. This sounds like a paradox, and would be one if Peter's behaviour had consisted merely in submitting to James's demands. But the manner in which Paul develops his argument against Peter shows that he regards the step taken by Peter from a quite different point of view as well.

The reproach against Peter runs as follows: εἰ σὺ Ἰουδαῖος ὑπάρχων ἐθνικῶς καὶ οὐκ Ἰουδαϊκῶς ζῇς, πῶς τὰ ἔθνη ἀναγκάζεις ἰουδαΐζειν; (2.14b). Certainly Paul's language here, and even more that in the following verses, already has in view his great justification of righteousness based on faith in contrast with the Galatians' keenness on circumcision. The transition from ch. 2 to ch. 3 is

---

Christian faction of extremists, but an urgent warning that the increasing rumours of Jewish-Christian fraternizing with uncircumcised Gentiles in Antioch and Galatia are now putting all the Jewish-Christian churches in Judea in considerable jeopardy from *non*-Christian Jews. In such circumstances S. Peter might well feel bound to do all he could to reduce the provocation.'

The description of the circumstances given by Schoeps is inconsistent. In *Paulus*, pp. 57ff., especially pp. 62f., he sees correctly that on the basis of Gal. 2.9f. one must speak of 'a genuine agreement' (p. 63) between Paul and James. Nevertheless he classes the τινὲς ἀπὸ Ἰακώβου of Gal. 2.12 with the Jerusalem extremists, whom James *resists*. But if the argument of Baur is not accepted for Gal. 2.1–10, then it must be abandoned for 2.11ff. as well.

[13] G. Kittel, *ZNW* 30, 1931, p. 152, rightly draws attention to this, though without having seen the correct reason for it.

[14] R. A. Lipsius, HCNT, p. 30.

[15] And of Barnabas whose behaviour no doubt stirred Paul more deeply than that of Peter. But in the context of Gal. 1f. he is naturally interested only in his dispute with *Peter*.

therefore, in fact, an imperceptible one. But this connexion of the two themes is surely only possible if the theme of chs. 3f. is found in some way also in the discussion with Peter. We cannot therefore have any doubt that Paul had it in mind when he denounced Peter in the terms reproduced in Gal. 2.14.

Many commentators do not notice the difficulty which this interpretation involves. Paul had certainly not hesitated to describe Peter's behaviour in blunt terms, saying that first he, then the other Jewish Christians, finally even Barnabas, separated themselves from the Gentile Christian community. But there is no word about encouraging or even forcing the Gentile Christians at the same time to accept the Law. That would indeed have been a plain breach of the Jerusalem agreement and much more serious than the mere withdrawal of the Jewish Christians. When describing Peter's behaviour Paul would have had to criticize such conduct above all else and most pungently. Yet he does not mention it, and when he explains Peter's behaviour as due to fear of men, it is evident how little he himself credits Peter with a *theological* change of mind, which might have let him urge the Law on the Gentiles. Nor could he possibly have characterized Peter's conduct with appropriate and sufficient severity as 'hypocrisy' if the latter had summoned the Gentile Christians to observe the Jewish Law.[16]

Consequently ἀναγκάζεις ἰουδαΐζειν can only mean 'indirect compulsion'.[17] Clearly Paul fears that, whatever the personal motives of Peter's conduct may be, his return to living under the Law could be understood by the Gentiles as a theological decision for justification through the Law. If Peter, the Christian, thinks that he can no longer live as a Gentile, then must not also the Christians from amongst the Gentiles think that they must live like Jews? Questioning such as this may be heard, and it is the possible effect on the Jewish Christians' decision suggested by this which makes Paul scandalized by Peter's behaviour. It is intelligible that Paul reacts thus sharply and why he does so.

Of course, the mere existence of Jewish-Christian churches

---

[16] So Lietzmann in *Kleine Schriften* II, p. 287.

[17] Sieffert, *Galater*, p. 137. T. Zahn, too, speaks of 'indirect' compulsion (*Galater*, p. 118). J. B. Lightfoot expresses himself the most clearly—as he often does—when he writes: 'ἀναγκάζεις, i.e. practically oblige them, though such was not his intention', *Galatians*, p. 114. Cf. also Munck, *Paul*, pp. 124f.

observing the Law confronts Paul with the general task of explaining to his Gentile-Christian congregations about the observance of the Law. But it is clear that this retreat of a great Jewish-Christian congregation under authoritative leadership within the most important church in the Gentile area from fellowship with the Gentile Christians must intensify the problem decisively; in addition, the reasons for this withdrawal, with its underlying tactical considerations—$\phi o \beta o \acute{u} \mu \epsilon \nu o s\ \tau o \grave{u} s\ \grave{\epsilon} \kappa\ \pi \epsilon \rho \iota \tau o \mu \hat{\eta} s$—were indeed adequate, but not particularly honourable. Barnabas, the missionary to the Gentiles, joined this party. Finally Antioch was still the headquarters of the mission to the Gentiles.

Thus Paul is not attacking Peter's personal decision in so far as it could be justified by the Jerusalem agreement; the fact of Peter's $\iota o \nu \delta a \acute{\iota} \zeta \epsilon \iota \nu$ is not in itself reprehensible—otherwise Paul's wrath would have fallen also on James and his envoys, indeed on the Jewish Christians as a whole, and even on the arrangement which Paul had made with them, and which took the $\iota o \nu \delta a \acute{\iota} \zeta \epsilon \iota \nu$ of Jewish Christians for granted. It was only the inconsistency of Peter's conduct in view of its ominous consequences for his churches which provoked his criticism. This fact explains the other details of Paul's line of argument without straining its meaning.

Paul emphasizes that he found fault with Peter $\emph{\check{\epsilon} \mu \pi \rho o \sigma \theta \epsilon \nu\ \pi \acute{a} \nu \tau \omega \nu}$. The object which Paul's account has in view supplies a sufficient reason for alluding to the circumstances in which the discussion took place: the apostle is showing that he was independent enough to charge Peter publicly with his offence. Of course, that cannot have been the primary reason for the publicity of what Paul did. Moreover, he certainly did not drag personal matters into the open out of spite. If he thought it necessary to attack Peter publicly, his purpose must have been to counteract any unpleasant public effects of the Jewish-Christian action. Thus it was, in fact, the public consequences of Peter's decision which provoked Paul's rebuke.

This is shown, too, by the pointed allusion to Barnabas, his fellow worker hitherto, whose participation in the behaviour of the Jewish Christians angered Paul particularly. It is not by chance that he is the only one besides Peter whom Paul mentions by name. We know that this dissension with Barnabas led to Paul seeking fresh companions for his missionary journeys—Silas, then Timothy. The account given us in Acts 15.36–41 certainly supplies a different motive for the breach between Paul and Barnabas, but can be understood only as a modification by Luke of the situation related by Paul in Gal. 2.13;[18] that is to say, Luke has turned a disagreement on a matter of principle into a personal quarrel.[19] The emphasis on Barnabas in Gal. 2.13 and the fact that Paul parted from him indicate afresh that the apostle regarded the significance of Peter's decision from the point of view of its consequences for his missionary work; after all, Barnabas had been his closest fellow worker, enjoying exactly the same authority. How could *his* decision in particular be made intelligible to the Gentile Christians. He had made himself impossible as Paul's colleague, even though—as one would like to assume—he might never have thought of living according to the Law outside Antioch and when engaged on his missionary work amongst the Gentiles.

If Paul in Gal. 2.11ff., too, shows himself to be particularly interested in giving an account of his dispute with Peter, yet there can be no doubt that his disagreement with Barnabas formed the real substance of that unfortunate incident in Antioch. A good part of his anger with Peter arose from the consequences which his behaviour forced upon Barnabas in particular. It is no accident that Luke reports only the dispute between Paul and *Barnabas*; it was this dispute which stamped the episode in Antioch upon the memory of Christendom.

Finally we must refer to the quality of ὑπόκρισις by which the Jewish-Christian conduct was characterized twice in Gal. 2.13. It can hardly be understood to mean 'hypocrisy', that is, that dissimulation in which visible behaviour does not agree with inner conviction. For the fear of the Jews which Paul gives as the motive of the Jewish Christians for separating themselves was certainly justified and in any case genuine.

It is more likely that Paul considered the dissimulation to consist in Peter's conduct being open to the interpretation that he sought salvation in righteousness according to the Law, although he had decided to observe the Law merely from fear of the Jews. In that case there would certainly have been no subjective

---

[18] Haenchen, pp. 421/416.
[19] Preuschen, *Die Apostelgeschichte*, p. 98.

dissimulation, since Peter by no means intended to give the impression that he wished to attain salvation through the Law. But the effect of his decision which Paul feared in 2.14b made it, in fact, appear objectively as dissimulation.

But probably ὑπόκρισις is simply intended to describe the inconsistency of Peter's behaviour: He behaves now in this way, now in that. Moreover, this is supported by ὀρθοποδέω, rarely attested elsewhere, meaning 'to walk straight',[20] which Paul declares Peter is not doing, and which is evidently in contrast with 'limping with two different opinions' (I Kings 18.21)[21] as Peter appears to be doing.[22] It was just this inconsistency which made his conduct so ambiguous and dangerous for Paul's missionary work. If Peter had consistently kept to the separate existence of the Jewish Christians in accordance with the interpretation of the Jerusalem arrangement, there would have been no grounds for criticism. Paul would have objected even less to his ἐθνικῶς ζῆν, for which Peter alone would have had to answer. It was his holding aloof from the Gentile Christians after the ἐθνικῶς ζῆν which first created the problem.

Whatever the precise meaning given to ὑποκρίνειν may be, it completely excludes the possibility that Peter made a breach with the Gentile-Christian church owing to a private decision against the doctrine of justification by faith. For in that case Paul would have had to reproach him not with dissimulation but with lapsing into unbelief, with giving up the Christian fellowship altogether.[23] That was not in the least Paul's intention. In spite of all his criticism he does not renounce his fellowship with Peter. This is seen also in the following difficult section, 2.15ff., which is directed not against Peter's false belief but against his inconsistency.

3. Occasionally[24] the attempt has been made to introduce a complete break after v. 14, and to consider vv. 15ff. as no longer part of what was said to Peter. So far as I know, none of the

[20] Verse 14; cf. Zahn, *Galater*, pp. 116f.; E. Meyer, *Ursprung*, p. 426, speaks correctly of Peter's 'inconsistency and indecision'.
[21] R. A. Lipsius, *Galater*, pp. 29f.
[22] Cf. on this G. D. Kilpatrick in *Neutestamentliche Studien für R. Bultmann* (BZNW 21), 1954, pp. 269–74.
[23] 'S. Paul could fairly describe such conduct, even with such motives, by the unpleasant word "hypocrisy"—whereas a reversion to strict Jewish principles on this matter, openly acknowledged, could not be so described with any justice' (Dix, *Jew and Greek*, pp. 43f.).
[24] See Zahn, *Galater*, p. 119.

modern commentators hold this opinion.[25] And they are right. Hence Paul is declaring to Peter: 'We are Jews by faith, not Gentile sinners. But because we know that no man is justified by works of the Law but through faith in Christ Jesus, we, too, have become believers in Christ Jesus in order that we might be justified by faith in Christ and not through works of the Law; for by works of the Law shall no one be justified.'[26]

That is Paul's doctrine of justification in a nutshell. It is obvious that Paul is writing not about past history with reference to Peter but about what is happening now with reference to the Galatians. But the substance of what he said to Peter cannot have been different from what he is here explaining to the Galatians; for Paul's statements could at any time be checked by his readers. Above all, his appeal to Peter on the strength of justification by grace as being the *common* ground of their faith must have corresponded to the contemporary situation.[27] In 2.15f. Paul has not yet started to argue, but is first preparing the ground for the argument which follows. There is one thing, so he assumes, on which we both agree, namely that the Jews, too, are not justified by the works of the Law, but by faith. The ἡμεῖς addressed to Peter necessarily includes him—in fact, the Peter who had again begun to live Ἰουδαϊκῶς.[28] This assumes that when Peter returned to the Law he by no means intended to follow the way of justification by the Law; and this again agrees with Paul's statement that Peter had parted company with the Gentile Christians from fear of men.

In view of this assumption which they hold in common, Peter's conduct must be deemed blameworthy. This appears from vv. 17f., which deal with Peter's actual conduct; for so far no reason

---

[25] Yet cf. B. Reicke in *Studia Paulina*, 1953, p. 175.

[26] The logical arrangement of the sentences is understood somewhat differently by H. Schlier, with whom P. Althaus agrees; against this R. Bultmann, 'Zur Auslegung von Gal. 2.15–18', pp. 41ff.

[27] We must reflect how impossible it was for the Jewish Christians in Palestine to admit that the Gentiles would obtain salvation apart from the Law through faith in Christ, whilst they regarded the Law as a necessary preliminary condition for the Jews to enter into the Kingdom of God. The recognition by the Jewish Christians of Palestine of the mission to the Gentiles which disregarded the Law had undoubtedly taken place, and this necessarily included relinquishing the Law as the means of salvation altogether, and thus for themselves as well. In I Cor. 15.11 Paul testifies otherwise than in Gal. 2, but even more explicitly, to the oneness of the preaching in Jerusalem and in the Pauline mission area.

[28] Sieffert, *Galater*, p. 146.

has yet been given why Peter's actions did not agree with the truth of the gospel: εἰ δὲ ζητοῦντες δικαιωθῆναι ἐν Χριστῷ εὑρέθημεν καὶ αὐτοὶ ἁμαρτωλοί, ἆρα Χριστὸς ἁμαρτίας διάκονος; μὴ γένοιτο.

Verses 17f. are unintelligible if it is not realized that the course of the argument culminates in these verses. Thus, for example, Schlier thinks that it is already brought to an end with v. 16 and regards vv. 17f. merely as the refutation of an objection by a Jewish-Christian opponent.[29] As though Paul could have concluded his argumentation against Peter by establishing their unanimity!

Accordingly Schlier paraphrases the objection in v. 17 as follows: If Christ declares a *sinner* to be justified, then, in fact, he encourages sin by abrogating the Law. Paul denies this by arguing in v. 18 that he who brings the Law into force again becomes a sinner. But I cannot understand how this last—correct—sentence proves that justification by grace does not encourage sin. Hence Schlier's understanding of this difficult passage is unsatisfying.

How must we understand it? To begin with it is essential to ask how εὑρέθημεν καὶ αὐτοὶ ἁμαρτωλοί is related to ζητοῦντες δικαιωθῆναι ἐν Χριστῷ. Is a man found to be a sinner *before*, or rather *at* his justification?[30] Of course he is, but Christ does not thereby become an agent of sin in the bad sense of the word implied in our passage. Does a man remain a sinner *in* and *owing to* his justification? That would be the opponent's objection to justification by grace, which is being rebutted according to Schlier; we saw that this interpretation breaks down when it comes to v. 18. Or does he become a sinner *through* his justification, as, for example, Lipsius[31] understands it, the abrogation of the Law luring the sinner into sin? But even so, v. 18 does not explain the μὴ γένοιτο. The same criticism must be levelled against Lietzmann's exegesis of this passage in *An die Galater*; he sees the Jewish objection underlying v. 17, namely that Christ moves away from the Law and therefore towards sin. Or does *Paul* say that even one who is justified still commits sin? But this idea would be quite un-Pauline, and, moreover, would not lead to the conclusion that in Christ an agent of

---

[29] *Galater*, pp. 59f.
[30] So Zahn, *Galater*, p. 126, who thinks that devout Jews, too, learn when they are justified that they are sinners; cf. Sieffert, p. 150.
[31] P. 32.

sin could be seen, quite apart from the fact that then, too, v. 18 does not fit in.

There remains only the possibility of understanding the sin described in v. 17 as meaning the actual attempt to become justified through Christ. That is also linguistically the most likely: if since, or rather because, we are seeking justification in Christ we are found to be sinners . . .; that is, if the way of justification by faith is itself sin. This is how Bultmann and Althaus also understand it.[32] Bultmann then continues in v. 17: ἄρα Χριστὸς ἁμαρτίας διάκονος = . . . then Christ is an agent of sin. The μὴ γένοιτο rejects this absurd sentence. Thus a satisfactory meaning is achieved. Since elsewhere in Paul μὴ γένοιτο always follows a question, it would be better to read: ἄρα Χριστὸς ἁμαρτίας διάκονος; That is what Althaus does: . . . is not Christ then an agent of sin? In that case it can certainly be only a rhetorical question, for under the supposed condition Christ is actually an agent of sin and the μὴ γένοιτο would again be refusing to admit the absurdity of a sentence leading to such a conclusion. The meaning is in both cases the same.

Bultmann now considers the sentence owing to its absurdity to be a way of expressing something unreal: If we *should be* found to be sinners. That is linguistically possible. But Bultmann, too, overlooks the real allusion in this sentence which is concerned with the dispute with Peter. He does not base his exegesis on 2.11–16, but on 2.20f. Yet in v. 17 Paul is attacking Peter's conduct directly. In what way? Now, we are told in v. 18 εἰ γὰρ ἃ κατέλυσα ταῦτα πάλιν οἰκοδομῶ, παραβάτην ἐμαυτὸν συνιστάνω. It is generally assumed that v. 18 is a parenthesis, whilst v. 19 continues the train of thought from v. 17.[33] The purpose of this parenthesis can only be to elucidate the meaning of v. 17 as part of the argument with Peter. But even without this assumption it is clear that v. 18 explains v. 17. In that case the παραβάτης of v. 18 corresponds to the ἁμαρτωλοί of v. 17. How does the παραβάτης show himself to be a sinner? He again puts into practice that which he had previously rejected. This proves that he was wrong in 'tearing it down'. The decision which he had cancelled—not the

---

[32] See Bultmann, 'Zur Auslegung von Gal. 2.15-18', and Althaus, *Die kleineren Briefe, ad loc.*
[33] Bultmann, Lietzmann, Schlier and others.

cancellation of the decision!—is regarded as being a transgression. But *Peter* had put into practice again that which he had already given up, namely the Law. It is *his* conduct which is described in vv. 17f.[34]

Paul is saying to him, 'Although we are Jews, we have put our faith in Jesus, because the works of the Law do not bring justification. But if the endeavour to be justified in Christ is sin, is Christ not then an agent of sin? Of course, that is impossible! But you, Peter, are making him one in effect, if you relinquish again the freedom from the Law which you had achieved and return to the works of the Law; for thereby you declare that by accepting this freedom you had acted as a sinner.'[35]

It seems to me quite open to question whether Paul simplified matters so much when arguing against Peter himself. For by this line of argument he imputes to him indirectly that when he returned once more to the Law he made a theological decision against justification by faith. Thus he equates the motive for Peter's decision with what he fears will be the *result* of this decision in the eyes of his churches, namely doubts about the validity of justification by faith. At the same time Paul knows that it was mere fear of men which determines Peter's decision. The solution of the problem was therefore not so simple as Paul represents it to be in 2.15–18. This may explain the tortuous method of his argument; yet it remains evident that Peter's vacillating behaviour, called 'hypocrisy', formed the real point of departure of Paul's criticisms.

---

[34] Althaus, p. 20.
[35] Althaus, who is right in seeing to what v. 18 really refers, interprets it thus: If Peter returns to the Law, he has not really been emancipated from it; but in that case, in Paul's view, his violation of it was in fact sinful. But Paul cannot possibly want to tell Peter that when he began to live without regard for the Law he was *in fact* behaving as a sinner!
On the other hand, Oepke is correct and his explanation of the passage is also reproduced by Schlier as being its possible meaning (in his view the less probable one): 'Therefore putting the Law into practice again after giving it up means nothing less than that Peter is acting in contradiction of his faith in Christ, that in retrospect he is branding that faith as a serious error', *Der Brief des Paulus an die Galater* (THKNT²), 1957, p. 61; H. Lietzmann, *Galater*, on this passage reproduces this interpretation, which he does not accept, as being the 'usual' one. J. Munck, *Paul*, p. 127, also sees that this must really be the meaning of the sentence and paraphrases it: '. . . as you (Peter) were when you were in Antioch, because you had sat at table with the Gentile Christians, and then when the Jerusalem brethren came felt in your conscience that you had acted wrongly—is Christ then an agent of sin?' However, he then prefers another rather abstruse explanation.

Moreover, Paul had, in fact, no interest in rehearsing the historical details. His account is 'tendentious' and in our section actually shows bias in two directions. First he wants to show his independence of Peter. He has done this already by his account of Peter being rebuked at all. But from v. 14 onwards the more this rebuke is developed the more its substance is expressed with an eye to the Galatians, whose hankering after the Law Paul must now discuss. It is to them that vv. 19–21, although still belonging by their form to what is said to Peter, are entirely addressed, as were the preceding verses, 17f., at least in what they tacitly implied, namely that Peter had vacillated from theological reasons in his attitude to the Law. For in Paul's view these are the only reasons for which the Galatians submit themselves to circumcision.

Paul could not report that Peter had resumed table-fellowship with the Gentiles. Therefore Peter had not done so; for Paul would not have passed over in silence the successful outcome of his disagreement with him.[36] Such a success was not to be expected. It is even doubtful whether Paul insisted on a success of this kind. What mattered to him was to make it clear publicly that, in spite of the attitude of the Jewish Christians in Antioch, justification is to be sought not through the works of the Law but in faith in Christ. Here Peter would hardly have contradicted him. On the other hand, Paul could not simply ignore the undoubtedly legitimate fear of Jewish retaliation which determined Peter's conduct, however unpleasant such wavering must have been to him.

As we have seen, Paul parted from Barnabas. He could not possibly carry on a Gentile mission with a Judaizing colleague. His conflict with Barnabas was certainly in every way more important than the dispute with Peter which Paul reports in detail. But none of the altercations indicate any fundamental withdrawal from fellowship in Christ. Paul always mentions Peter as well as Barnabas quite naturally as members of the one Christian Church (Gal. 1.18; 2.7f.; I Cor. 9.5f.; 15.5); he includes the party of Peter, that is, the Jewish Christians who observed the Law, in the Corinthian church as a matter of course (I Cor. 1.12; 3.22).[37]

[36] Haenchen, pp. 422/417.
[37] Cf. Schmithals, *Die Gnosis in Korinth*, pp. 164ff.

That would be impossible if the fellowship of faith in Christ's righteousness which united Paul and Peter had been broken by the affair in Antioch. This fellowship had never been brought directly into the discussion; nor had the agreement of Jerusalem ever been called in question in the least, still less cancelled, by the unhappy incident in Antioch.

IV

THE COLLECTION OF THE CONTRIBUTIONS

ONE of the stipulations made at the 'Apostolic Council' was the obligation undertaken by Paul to remember the 'poor' (Gal. 2.10). In K. Holl's well-known essay,[1] he has attempted to prove that these contributions were a *legal* levy by the church of Jerusalem. That is not impossible, but it cannot be proved. It is certain that Paul did not understand this obligation to be a legal one, whatever its intention.[2]

Even if the Jerusalem church had regarded the contributions as an indication that the legal sovereignty of their church had been recognized, this would only have made even more evident what the collection as a moral and religious obligation showed clearly enough: namely, the desire to cling to the unity of the Church. It chimes in with this that the other arrangement, the separation of the mission areas, was intended not to break up the unity of the Church, but on the contrary to make it possible in view of the risk which the church in Palestine ran from the Jews.

Paul asserts in Gal. 2.10 that he had taken great pains to assist the indigent church in Jerusalem. The truth of this statement is verified by such passages as Rom. 15.25–32; I Cor. 16. 1–4; II Cor. 8f. Moreover, the collection of the contributions had given him much trouble in Corinth and Thessalonica, since his opponents used it as a pretext to reproach Paul with personal covetousness: I Cor. 12.14–18;[3] I Thess. 2.5–12.[4] Yet Paul carried it through. He wants to convey the proceeds himself to Jerusalem (Rom. 15.25–32). He gives this as the sole purpose of his journey thither (Rom. 15.25). Therefore he cares a great deal about unity

---

[1] 'Der Kirchenbegriff des Paulus in seinem Verhältnis zu dem der Urgemeinde', *SBA*, 1921, pp. 920–47 = *Gesammelte Aufsätze* II, pp. 44–67.
[2] II Cor. 8.14; Rom. 15.27.
[3] Schmithals *Die Gnosis in Korinth*, pp. 29ff.; *Apostelamt*, pp. 205ff.
[4] For this I refer to my essay on 'Die historische Situation der Thessalonicherbriefe' in *Paulus und die Gnostiker*.

with the Jewish Christians of Palestine to which the gift of his churches testifies.[5]

The whole treatment of the business of collection would normally permit but one conclusion, that the relations between Paul and Jerusalem are altogether happy. According to Gal. 2.10 the only possible assumption is that the same mutual understanding which led to the Gentile-Christian charitable aid being arranged still made itself felt when the gift was collected and handed over. But then Rom. 15.30f. seems to contradict this. There Paul asks the Roman Christians to pray for him ἵνα ῥυσθῶ ἀπὸ τῶν ἀπειθούντων ἐν τῇ Ἰουδαίᾳ καὶ ἡ διακονία μου ἡ εἰς Ἱερουσαλὴμ εὐπρόσδεκτος τοῖς ἁγίοις γένηται. Lietzmann[5a] infers from this sentence that the opposition of the Jerusalem church to the Gentile-Christian community was inconceivably bitter, in spite of the 'Apostolic Council'. Not all the commentators attach so bitter a meaning as Lietzmann to what is stated in Rom. 15.30f. about the relationship between Paul and the primitive church in Jerusalem, but I have not found anywhere a fundamentally different understanding of these words.[6]

Now, this way of understanding them lands us in difficulties. It is evident that Paul does not hint at such tensions elsewhere, and his treatment of the matter of the collection really excludes them. But if such tensions existed and the contributions were possibly unwelcome, why does he collect them with so much zeal and why does he make a special journey to Jerusalem at all, although everything is urging him to go through Rome to Spain, where the Gentiles are certainly not likely to ask him about his relations with the Christians in Jerusalem?

Moreover, for what reason should the Jerusalem church shut the door on Paul together with his contributions? What a catastro-

---

[5] The theological significance of the contributions should not be underrated. It was more than an act of love. What R. Schnackenburg ('Die Kirche im Neuen Testament', *Quaestiones Disputatae* 14, 1961, p. 75) writes about it seems to me very pertinent: 'By this means Paul becomes the preacher and teacher of Christian concord in all his churches, and beyond this also the promoter of harmony between the mother church of Jerusalem and its newly founded churches (a large collection!). Thereby he made an essential contribution to the development of a consciousness of a universal Church, both theologically and practically. The main credit for the fact that the rapidly spreading Church did not break up from within is, humanly speaking, due to Paul's theology, which made all believers actively conscious of their oneness, given to them by God and calling them imperatively to unity. . . .'

[5a] *Römer*, p. 123.

[6] The most recent in E. Lohse, 'Glaube und Werke', *ZNW* 48, 1957, p. 18.

phic turn must things have taken after the 'Apostolic Council', indeed after Gal. 2.1–10 was written; for in the letter to the Galatians Paul describes the arrangements of the 'Apostolic Council' as still valid.[7] The refusal of an urgently needed delivery of money, especially if it was intended to be understood as a dutiful tribute to their central authority, presupposes such a complete disruption of comradeship that one is extremely reluctant to assume it merely on the basis of Rom. 15.30f.

Finally, Paul was received by the Jerusalem church by no means in an unfriendly manner. That can be learned from the account in Acts, however great the caution with which it is accepted.[8] What makes Paul expect a hostile reception?

But is not Rom. 15.31 so unequivocal that all doubts must be set aside on account of the plain wording of the text? By no means! On the contrary! In order to make it possible to understand the passage in the traditional way the commentators are accustomed actually to make an alteration tacitly in the text. It is true that in doing so they merely follow the Textus Receptus, which is contradicted by all the good witnesses of the text. In this text another ἵνα is interpolated between καί and ἡ διακονία. Without accepting this late reading, Lipsius, Lietzmann, Michel and many others nevertheless translate it in the sense of the Textus Receptus: 'I appeal to you . . . to strive together with me in your prayers to God on my behalf that I may be delivered from the unbelievers in Judea, and that my service which takes me to Jerusalem may be acceptable to the saints.' Thus Paul's words certainly hardly leave any doubt that he fears two dangers in Jerusalem: the *Jews* might subject him to the fate of Stephen; the *Christians* might 'bluntly refuse' to accept the contributions and hence, of course, to receive Paul.[9]

But Paul had written something quite different: 'Pray for me that I may be delivered from the unbelievers in Judea and my

---

[7] One can make do—like Haenchen, pp. 549/544—with the hypothesis that meanwhile Paul's 'battle with the Judaizers' had been joined; but in that case it must at the same time be explained how Paul, whilst in the midst of the battle with Judaistic 'servants' of Satan' and 'false apostles', was gathering contributions just for these very people and their backers in Jerusalem from the communities they were attacking and was bringing these contributions personally to Jerusalem. This explanation is due from everyone.

[8] Haenchen, pp. 542ff./537ff.; see below, pp. 85ff.

[9] Haenchen, pp. 549/544.

service for Jerusalem be acceptable to the saints.' If the traditional way of understanding this statement were correct, the interpolated ἵνα would certainly only serve to make it clearer. The clarification would in that case even be necessary, as the above commentators rightly feel; for Paul's wording lets it be understood that he is affected by *one* fear and that the menace from the Jews is connected with the possible rejection of the contributions: 'Pray that the Jews do not harm me and (therefore) my contributions are welcome to the Christians.'

But does such a connexion exist? Certainly, and Haenchen has already described it exactly—from quite another point of view and certainly without fully drawing out the consequences of what he has recognized. He writes: 'Paul's visit occurred a few years before the murder by the Jews of James' the Lord's brother. The Jerusalem church was already then struggling for the last chance of missionary work in Israel. If it accepted Paul's contributions, then it was declaring in the eyes of the Jews its solidarity with him. This threatened to destroy the possibility of its own mission. This is overlooked by every commentator who lets James and the elders accept Paul's contributions joyfully.'[10]

What Haenchen has perspicaciously detected in the case of a single statement of Paul corresponds precisely with what our whole study up till now has discovered to be the situation which determined the complicated nature of Paul's relations to James, namely the relationship of the Jewish Christians to the Palestinian Jews. If legal proceedings were taken against Paul in Judea, then every evidence of mutural understanding between Paul and James' church would bring about not only frustration of the Jewish-Christian missionary efforts but also the persecution of the Jewish Christians. That would apply particularly if on the Jewish side the contributions were regarded rightly or wrongly as a tribute to the governing body of the church of Jerusalem, which by accepting this tribute indicated that it was responsible for Paul's activity. The more sharply the Jews reacted to Paul's arrival the less welcome to the Jewish Christians could the contributions be which Paul brought them, however gladly they would have liked to accept them; therefore the greater the danger also to the labour of love undertaken with so much trouble and sacrificial willingness

[10] P. 550/544.

The Collection of the Contributions

by Paul and his churches for the Jewish Christians[11]—and *vice versa*. There is thus every justification for the anxiety about the acceptance of his contributions in view of the hostility of the Jews expressed by Paul in Rom. 15.31.[12]

Consequently Rom. 15.30f. does not force us to revise the conception gained so far about the relationship between Paul and the Jewish Christians, nor need we in order to retain it assume a catastrophic deterioration in this relationship during the last part of the so-called third missionary journey.[13] On the contrary, this

---

[11] Paul was received by the Jews as badly as possible. Was the church in Jerusalem spared? After Acts 21.25, even before Paul's arrest, it disappears completely from Luke's account. There are several explanations for this. One of them might be: The church did not remain unmolested, and because Luke suppresses so far as possible the differences between Jews and Christians, he makes no further mention of the church. Then the striking failure to mention the collection might also be connected with this, if, as Paul feared according to Rom. 15.31, it did actually result in trouble for the church. According to Acts 24.17 the fact of the journey with the contributions does not seem to have been unknown to Luke. Another reason for the failure to mention it is given by Haenchen, pp. 550f./545.

[12] When Paul is writing I Cor. 16.1–4 about a year before his last visit to Jerusalem, he does not yet know whether he will once more go to see the church in Jerusalem before his journey to the West. When he comes to Corinth he intends to supply messengers with credentials and to send them to Jerusalem with the contributions collected in Corinth (and elsewhere). 'If it seems advisable that I should go also, they will accompany me' (I Cor. 16.4). We can only infer to what ἐὰν δὲ ἄξιον ᾖ refers. Paul will hardly have let his visit to Jerusalem depend on the amount of the contributions. Is he waiting for special guidance from God? But that would have to be expressed clearly as in I Cor. 4.19: ἐὰν ὁ κύριος θελήσῃ. Rom. 15.31 suggests the inference that he is undecided whether to travel to Jerusalem himself owing to the situation there. Therefore when writing I Cor. he is still waiting for news from Jerusalem whether his visit is expedient or is on the contrary unwelcome, because he does not want to be a burden to the church there nor to imperil his own life. In that case we should conclude from Rom. 15.31 that the Jerusalem church did not dissuade him from coming, yet without being able to banish his misgivings about his personal safety and the success of his mission to Jerusalem.

[13] Klein, 'Verleugnung', p. 321, thinks that the problem can be solved only if we assume 'that since the Council in Jerusalem a transference of power had taken place, in fact that Peter who favoured the undertaking of the contributions had been succeeded by James who was more intransigent about it.' But this is hardly a solution at all. For why does Paul take so much trouble about the contributions if the recipients do not want them in the least and had long ago rejected the whole Jerusalem agreement, which included amongst other matters the duty of making contributions? Moreover, according to the account in Gal. 2, James was already at the head of the Jerusalem authorities at the time of the 'Apostolic Council'; therefore he cannot have taken Peter's place afterwards.

Klein admittedly considers Paul's account in Gal. 2 to be unhistorical in this respect; he thinks that Peter was still playing the leading role alone at the time of the 'Apostolic Council', that James only came to the fore and was reckoned amongst the δοκοῦντες later. But here one untenable hypothesis is built on another. For Paul cannot possibly have misrepresented actual facts so completely in Gal. 2.

My criticism with regard to this question (*Apostelamt*, p. 75 n. 133) is rejected by Klein, who points to the joint responsibility of John and James for the agreement as far back as the 'Apostolic Council' ('Verleugnung', pp. 318f.). But it is unfortu-

conception is confirmed if Rom. 15.30f. is read without being encumbered by the Tübingen hypothesis according to which Paulinism and Judaizing must be assumed to be two fundamentally irreconcilable opposites throughout primitive Christian writings.

---

nate, and also disastrous for this thesis, that, though James and John are not reckoned amongst those who were considered important during the Council, they are made responsible for the agreements reached at that time. And did James assent responsibly to Peter's agreement in order to disavow it with Peter after he had pushed him into second place amongst the Jerusalem authorities?

Besides, I had written: In addition the hypothesis does not at all achieve what it is intended to achieve. It should explain in particular v. 6, which it accordingly paraphrases: 'Those who are *today* reputed to be something—that *then* they were nothing makes no difference to me, God shows no partiality—those who are *now* of repute added nothing to me *then*.' It is obvious that such a statement about which certainly no one will disagree with Paul is meaningless and ridiculous as an apology. Moreover, οἱ δοκοῦντες in v. 6 can be understood only as it is in v. 2 and v. 9, hence 'those who were of repute *then*'.

Whilst Klein does not deal with the latter decisive objection, he replies to the preceding one: 'It is precisely the present universally conspicuous position of authority of the "pillars" led by James which might provoke the Galatian opponents to say that Paul depended especially on them' (*op. cit.*, pp. 318f.). But this only increases the absurdity. For now Paul's opponents must have reproached him with depending on authorities, who (according to Klein) were at that time by no means the authorities; and Paul, instead of defending himself against misrepresentation of the actual historical facts, is said to have declared this misrepresentation in the parenthesis of v. 6 explicitly as of no account, although the accusation against him rested on this misrepresentation alone.

Finally, if Klein considers that his proposal is the only possible one for solving the problems in Gal. 2.1–10, I am unable to share such pessimism. The ἦσαν in the decisive v. 6 possibly refers to the fact that at the time of the letter to the Galatians the circle of the δοκοῦντες or of the στῦλοι, as such, no longer existed. John's brother James had suffered a martyr's death, Peter was (v. 7) at work as a missionary outside Jerusalem, and the position of James, the Lord's brother, was therefore also no longer that of one of the three δοκοῦντες, whatever it might have been formerly. The emphasis in the parenthesis in v. 6 does not in fact lie on the ἦσαν, but on the ὁποῖοί ποτε, and accordingly v. 6 means: those who were of some importance—what importance it was does not interest me, for it is of no importance to God—added nothing to me. Hence we are concerned in the parenthesis with a typical Pauline remark.

V

PAUL'S LAST VISIT TO JERUSALEM

1. WE turn now to the account of Paul's reception in Jerusalem in Acts 21.15–26. This account need, of course, occupy our attention only if we can with some confidence consider it to be historical. So it is necessary to say something about the sources of the Acts.[1] All commentators are agreed that the author of Acts had at his disposal good material for describing some parts of the Pauline missionary activity. There are many indications that he possessed a consecutive source with information about it. Dibelius in his essays on the Acts has frequently stated that this source was an itinerary, that is, a record of the stopping-places on his travels. 'It appears that this itinerary also contained comments upon the apostles' reception, their hosts, their activities and the results.'[2] Dibelius regarded the *Sitz im Leben* of this itinerary—he speaks of it only in passing—as lying in the fact that 'For practical reasons an account of this kind would have to be used on such journeys in order that if the journey were to be repeated the way and former hosts could be found once more.'[3] Recently G. Schille[4] has rightly raised objections to this view. The picture of Paul's missionary work, which an itinerary originating in this way presupposes, conflicts with everything which we know for certain about Pauline missionary activity. Besides, the itinerary, even within the restricted limits given to it by Dibelius, goes far beyond a record for such a practical purpose. It has a definite literary quality. So it looks as if the itinerary were in Dibelius's view a single piece of a literary type. Again Schille[5] is correct in bringing out that we have no other example of such a literary type. These

---

[1] Cf. Haenchen, 13th ed., pp. 72–80.
[2] Dibelius, *Acts*, p. 104, cf. pp. 69f.
[3] P. 126; cf. pp. 210f.
[4] 'Die Fragwürdigkeit eines Itinerars der Paulusreisen', *TLZ* 84, 1959, cols. 165ff., especially col. 174.
[5] *Op. cit.*, col. 174.

points suffice to demonstrate how precarious it is to postulate an itinerary as a source of Acts.

What is to be done now? Shall we, as Schille proposes, explain by 'a reference to Luke's literary ability'[6] what hitherto seemed to be explained by the hypothesis of the itinerary? The material used by Luke is completely incompatible with this, and hardly anything of what appears to come from the 'itinerary' can be explained by Luke's literary motives which are recognizable in the other sections of Acts.[7]

The way out of this dilemma is to be sought in the opposite direction. 'It is one of the characteristics of the missionary aretologies of antiquity to string a number of individual stories on to the thread of an apostle's wanderings.'[8] These missionary aretologies are parallelled in other ancient travel literature.[9] In these, as Norden shows, the 'I' or 'we' style is often alternated with narrative in the third person.[10] The source which we wrongly call an itinerary also belongs to this literary type. It was more than a list of halting-places. Only Luke has often let the abrupt statements about these places on the journey remain with little alteration, so that they stand out conspicuously in his book and could easily give rise to the itinerary hypothesis. He has on, the other hand, dealt very freely with the narrative material of the missionary report and made it to a considerable extent serve his own style of recording the events. Therefore it is impossible to reconstruct Luke's source in detail.[11]

This conception of the source problem in the Pauline portion

---

[6] *Op. cit.*, col. 174.

[7] Cf. Haenchen, 13th ed., pp. 14*.

[8] G. Bornkamm, *Mythos und Legende in den apokryphen Thomas-Akten* (FRLANT 49), 1933, p. 2.

[9] E. Norden, *Agnostos Theos*⁴, 1956, pp. 313–27. Although we are justified in rejecting the untenable theory of the sources of Acts worked out by Norden, yet we must not overlook whatever serviceable ancient material he collected.

Cf. also the important study of R. Söden, *Die apokryphen Apostelgeschichten und die romanhafte Literatur der Antike*, 1932; R. Reizenstein, *Hellenistische Wundererzählungen*², 1963, *passim*.

[10] There are no grounds for Haenchen's opinion that the itinerary and the 'we' 'had nothing to do with each other' (pp. 434f./429f.). The so-called 'we' source is a component part of the so-called 'itinerary'. Cf. Conzelmann in his review of Haenchen's commentary in *TLZ* 85, 1960, col. 244. Haenchen now no longer maintains the above-mentioned opinion; see the next note.

[11] Cf. Haenchen, 'Das "Wir" in der Apostelgeschichte und das Itinerar', *ZTK* 58, 1961, pp. 329–66, especially p. 366. The conclusions of this important essay suffer nevertheless in my opinion from the fact that the author starts from the hypothesis that 'Luke' had an itinerary in front of him, instead of first testing this hypothesis.

of the Acts cannot be demonstrated in detail here, but it will hold good for the section, Acts 21.15–26.

2. Verses 15–18 of this section are generally and for sound reasons considered to be a more or less verbatim reproduction of the older travel report. Perhaps v. 19 also still belongs to this source and Acts 15.4, 12 may have been shaped in accordance with it. But from v. 20 Luke is undoubtedly speaking himself, of course also on the basis of a source. The whole story in 21.20–27 cannot be just a fabrication. This is supported by the fact, amongst many others, that the account which Luke gives in vv. 23ff. of the cultic rite attributed to Paul remains essentially unintelligible. A Nazirite order which Paul joins for seven days does not exist.[12] Yet we can well accept Luke's account as a partially understood reproduction of a prototype.[13] Moreover, the record of the journey can hardly have ended with the arrival in Jerusalem, especially as it had contained earlier allusions to the arrest which was to be expected (Acts 21.4, 10ff.).[14] Consequently Luke reproduced his source in a version of his own.

A typically Lucan trait, for instance, is the statement in v. 20 that there are among the Jews many tens of thousands of those who have believed. This is a boundless exaggeration which is particularly noticeable when we observe that according to v. 22 all these tens of thousands are supposed to live in Jerusalem.[15] Luke, of course, takes this number for granted; for, after all, in the earliest period he lets 3,000 members be added to the Church by baptism in one day (Acts 2.41).

According to v. 17, Paul and his companions were received gladly by 'the brethren' on their arrival in Jerusalem. That does not mean that the whole church appeared to receive Paul; but it is certainly not implied that the 'brethren' were 'primarily Hellenists'.[16] It can only mean that the Jerusalem church as such received Paul gladly through its members present in Mnason's house. It

---

[12] There is a good discussion of this question in Haenchen, pp. 546ff./540ff.; how little Luke knew about the nature of the Nazirite rule appears forcibly also in Acts 18.18 (see p. 96).

[13] Haenchen, pp. 548f./542f.

[14] See in addition Haenchen, p. 548/542.

[15] According to the calculation of J. Jeremias, Jerusalem had during Roman times a population of about 25,000 ('Die Einwohnerzahl Jerusalems zur Zeit Jesu', *Zeitschrift des Deutschen Palästina-Vereins*, 1943, pp. 24–31).

[16] R. Knopf in *Die Schriften des NT*², 1907, I, p. 632; so also Haenchen, pp. 544/538; W. Beyer, p. 129; cf. H. H. Wendt, *Die Apostelgeschichte, ad loc.*

agrees with this that on the following day the leaders of this church were already assembled when Paul with his companions visited James: the conference had already been arranged on the preceding day (21.18). It does *not* agree with this that according to v. 22 the church in Jerusalem does not yet know about Paul's arrival. But this contradiction cannot be removed by the explanation just mentioned that the brethren in v. 17 must be considered the adherents of an exclusively Hellenist group in the church.[17] For the ignorance of the church about Paul's arrival cannot, after all, be reconciled with the fact that the elders of the church had already been called together for a conference with Paul.[18] Hence the hand of Luke can be felt in v. 22 as well.

Now, Luke's description in vv. 20ff. arouses misgivings on basic matters, too. Were the Jewish Christians of Jerusalem really ζηλωταὶ τοῦ νόμου? Everything that we have ascertained so far tells against this. They observed the Law, but were not zealous for it. If nevertheless Luke is describing the Jerusalem church correctly, the question remains: For what reason would Paul have had to show it proof of his—non-existent—fidelity to the Law? Was there, in fact, any physical danger on the part of the Jewish Christians from which the friendly elders of these Christians wished to protect him? What a foolish idea! According to Luke's account the leaders of the church are in any case convinced that the rumours branding Paul as an antinomian agitator amongst the Jews in the Diaspora are incorrect. How, then, can the church as a whole believe them? Therefore we cannot accept Luke's description.

Attempts have been made to solve these difficulties by means of literary criticism: 'The words of the church members are not at all strange if they refer to Jews and not to Jewish Christians. Hence objections are raised to πεπιστευκότων in v. 20.'[19] This solution is analogous to the antiquated method of assuming throughout Acts

---

[17] Even the existence of such a group is very improbable. For after the persecution of Stephen it is unlikely that conditions for the Hellenists would have improved so much that the broken community could be gathered together again. On the contrary! The death of both the one and the other James, and the flight of the Christians from Jerusalem before the Jewish revolt, show that as time passed the position also of the 'Hebrews' in Jerusalem became more and more untenable.

[18] Cf. also Munck, *Paul*, pp. 239ff.

[19] E. Preuschen, *Die Apostelgeschichte*, p. 126, following F. C. Baur, *Paulus*, 1845, p. 200, and followed by Munck, p. 240, E. Schwartz, A. D. Nock, and others.

a source with comments and of reconstructing this source by omitting the additions. But the account in Acts 21.19–26 is a literary unity. Yet Preuschen was right in seeing that the historical issue of the conference between Paul and the church leaders must have been such that the reaction to be expected on the part of the Jews was pointed out to the apostle; that is, just that reaction which he himself already feared according to Rom. 15.31. The tension between vv. 17f. and v. 22 must then be ascribed to Luke, who has not quite fitted the source material admitted in vv. 17f. into his modified description of the historical events.

The substance of the formulation of the reproach against Paul in v. 21 goes back undoubtedly to the source: 'You teach all the Diaspora Jews to forsake Moses, telling them not to circumcise their children nor observe the customs.' For 21.28 shows Luke's wording.[20] It was exactly this accusation on the part of the Jews which the Jewish Christians were bound to fear when they included Paul in their fellowship. They were aware of this at the latest since the persecution of Stephen's community. The fear of this accusation led to the agreement of the 'Apostolic Council' in which Paul relinquished the mission to the Jews. It was also the same fear which led Peter (φοβούμενος τοὺς ἐκ περιτομῆς) on the urging of James to resume the separate life of the Jewish Christians in Antioch.

There can be no doubt that the Jewish authorities in Jerusalem were as well informed about Paul's activities as about the conditions in the Jerusalem church. It follows certainly from what was said above on pp. 47ff., that the accusation against Paul in the form reproduced in v. 21 was not justified.[21] James and the elders rightly proceed from the fact that Paul had not preached the rejection of the Law to the Jews (but the gospel to the Gentiles), in accordance with the agreement of Gal. 2.9. However, it is not particularly surprising that such an accusation could, in fact, be brought against Paul. No doubt Jews, too, attached themselves to Paul's churches, and these had thereby given up the observance of

---

[20] See pp. 27f.
[21] Cf. in addition J. Weiss, *Apostelgeschichte*, p. 36: 'That this accusation against Paul was really unjust must quite frankly be conceded, so it appears to me. For there seems to be no possible doubt that Paul neither preached freedom from the Law to the *Jews*, nor advised Jewish Christians not to circumcise their children. Nor can it be doubted that it must have been a matter of concern to Paul to refute prejudices of this kind.'

the Law if they had not done so already earlier; certainly many of these Jews had also given up letting their children be circumcised.[22] It is only to be expected that these cases would be represented as the successes of the anti-Jewish propaganda of the hated apostate Paul.[22a]

But this could not be a matter of indifference to the Jewish-Christian church. They had to attempt to divest themselves of the accusations against Paul if they did not wish to remain aloof from him—and his contributions! Before we examine this attempt we must ask why Luke re-arranged the historical facts so far as to represent the Jewish Christians themselves in place of the Jews as being those who were zealously concerned for the Law to be fulfilled. After what has been said, it should be clear that this is the case. This is corroborated beyond all shadow of doubt by the fact that it was not the Jewish Christians who laid their hands on Paul, but the Jews. The answer to our question is to be found in Luke's bias which we have already noticed and discussed earlier, whereby the Christian church is represented as the true Judaism.[23] This bias, which pervades the whole of the Acts, will be carried so far as to make Paul appear before the Council as a paragon of obedience to the Law: Acts 23.1ff.; 24.14ff.; 26.4ff. The historical record which presupposed a tension unwelcome to Luke between Jews and Jewish Christians thus gave place in Acts 21.19–26 to a narrative making the Jewish Christians the advocates of Pharisaism.[24] This transformation of the narrative gave Luke no more trouble than Preuschen was disposed to take when he wished to reconstruct the historical record by deleting two words.[25] Of course, we must not ask Luke whether he was not himself struck by the improbability of the report which he has given us.

3. After what has been said it can be considered certain that Paul had to clear himself before the Jews from the accusation made

---

[22] See pp. 54ff.

[22a] Cf. W. Foerster, 'Die δοκοῦντες', 289: . . . 'The fears of the primitive Church arose not from Paul's preaching to the Gentiles, but from the rumour that he was taking the gospel to the Jewish Christians.'

[23] See p. 32, n. 65; cf. also H. Conzelmann, *The Theology of St Luke*, pp. 147f.

[24] In addition Luke's account—and this is of special importance to the author—turns Palestine into a half-Christian country!

[25] This deletion, proposed already by F. C. Baur, has been accepted also by Bultmann, amongst others, and recently also by Munck (*Paul*, pp. 240ff.), who adopted and substantiated it—assessing correctly the historical position, but failing to appreciate the literary quality of Acts.

against him. Doubts are always being felt whether he attempted to do so in the way described by Luke. We have already pointed out that Haenchen has shown up the essential impossibility of the account given of it. This presupposes the misunderstanding of a source which according to Haenchen's hypothesis described how Paul first purified himself from the levitical defilement acquired by his having lived abroad,[26] in order to take part afterwards in the ceremony releasing four Nazirites from their vow and to pay their expenses. If this were so, the *source* would therefore already have told about Paul's observance of the Law in this case.[27] This source is reliable. We could then see the connexion between the contributions collected for the Jerusalem poor and the financial help to the poor Nazirites and could let this connexion supply the reason for Paul's being required to show proof in *this* manner that he on no account forbade Jews to keep the Law.

Now Haenchen's thesis is no more than an attempt—although a skilful one—to solve the problems of our passage, and as such it is no compelling proof that Paul actually behaved in the manner ascribed to him. Yet I find it hard to see how Luke's account can be explained if it has no historical foundation. That Luke invented this complicated story is an impossible hypothesis, particularly in view of his method of going to work. And we can also hardly assume that here he is following an unhistorical rumour—the origin of which would require to be explained—although he was following at least as far as 21.18 an excellent source; for then the whole scene of the uproar in the temple and of the arrest outside the temple would be unhistorical. Besides, as we saw, the traces in 21.20ff. of traditions agreeing with the source must not be overlooked,[28] and this source cannot have contained anything completely different from what Luke accepts from it for his account.

Only the most serious doubts about Luke's description of Paul's behaviour could induce us to reject Luke's report com-

---

[26] Billerbeck II, pp. 758ff.
[27] It is true that Paul himself made no vow nor did he offer any sacrifice for himself. Jerusalem was not so much concerned with Paul's personal behaviour regarding the Law, but rather with his attitude to the observance of the Law by the Jews by birth who had been admitted into the Christian Church.
[28] I should also like to attribute to the influence of the source the fact that in Acts 21 the twelve apostles, who up till then dominated the scene in Jerusalem, have suddenly disappeared and only James appears with the elders.

pletely. I do not know what kind of doubts these might be. Of course, we ought not interpret Paul's behaviour, as Luke does, as a sign that he himself lived in loyalty to the Law (21.24).[29] It was merely Paul's wish and duty to demonstrate by his behaviour that he by no means required the Jews and the Jewish Christians to abandon obedience to the Law. In fact, he had never required this. We need only recall again the agreement of the 'Apostolic Council' at which he explicitly accepted Peter's mission to the Jews which observed the Law. But if he considered it to be a possibility, or even a duty (I Cor. 7.18f.), for a Jewish Christian to remain within the Jewish nation as established by the Law, provided that the Law was not considered, as it was by the Pharisees, to be the means of salvation,[30] then he could not think that he was prohibited from observing a legal rite himself, if it served a useful purpose and could be done without endangering his preaching. He explicitly acknowledges that such is his practice: 'To the Jews I became as a Jew, in order to win Jews; to those under the law I became as one under the law—though not being myself under the law—that I might win those under the law' (I Cor. 9.20). When ought he to have applied this principle, if not under the circumstances of his last stay in Jerusalem? In the conditions prevailing in Jerusalem, an antinomianism based on principle would have been the best way of ensuring failure to win a single Jew; but it was his deepest longing—although he was himself only a missionary to the Gentiles—that his fellow countrymen, too, might confess Jesus as the Christ (Rom. 9–11).

Moreover, it was a very mild case of legal observance to redeem a few Nazirites after a cultic purification; for this proceeding

[29] H. J. Holtzmann, *Die Apostelgeschichte, ad loc.*, is quite right in seeing that the whole of Acts 21.20–26 tells of an act of confession, not of accommodation. There is widespread inclination to regard this section as a source with comments, and this told against the reliability of the record; for the deletion of the last seven words of v. 24 could not make the source credible. A correct interpretation of Holtzmann's remark shows that the whole account in its literary form is due to Luke, who transformed the act of accommodation into an act of confession.

[30] Of course, there is no question here of abnormally strict Jewish existence. The bulk of the Jewish nation were not at all inclined to Pharisiasm. The high standards required by righteousness according to the Law were far from being within the reach of everyone. But even the accursed *am haaretz*, which could not be righteous in the eyes of the Law, yet observed the Law. There was no other way of living as a Jew among Jews. Paul could have no hesitation about retaining this practical understanding of the Law for Jewish Christians, the majority of whom certainly did not come from Pharisaic circles. They belonged to the *am haaretz*, as the anti-Pharisaic bias of the synoptic tradition demonstrates.

could be regarded as an act of charity rather than understood as a measure of personal submission to the Law.

The question still remains—and here lies the most serious objection—whether Paul's behaviour does not render him guilty of the same hypocrisy with which he reproaches Peter in Antioch with so much indignation. But, if we have taken the right view of the matter, it was the possible effects of Peter's decision on the Gentile-Christian churches which for Paul gave importance to this decision, not Peter's action as such; effects of this kind were not be be feared in Jerusalem. But the reprehensible conduct of the Antiochene Jewish Christians consisted above all in their separating themselves from the Gentile Christians. Paul would never have considered it blameworthy if during the period when they sat at table with the Gentiles they had on their part in other respects observed the customs prescribed by the Law as well. Presumably this had also occurred, as we saw. Paul, on the other hand, whilst having no intention of giving up his own freedom from the Law, does no more than to show by his action that he does not forbid the Law to be observed. If the apostle is not thought capable of this, it is implied that he finds his salvation not in obedience to the Law but in freedom from the Law, whilst, in fact, he finds it in Christ, who demands such love to one's brother that even Christian freedom can be relinquished (I Cor. 8–10).

4. In this connexion we must examine two other statements in Acts which raise the same problems as those we have just considered. In Acts 16.1–3 we are told that Timothy of Lystra joined Paul as a fellow worker on his journey through Lycaonia, but that first Paul circumcised him.

The commentators are perfectly right in not disputing the fact that the narrative about Timothy reveals reliable traditions. Whilst 16.4f. certainly betrays Luke's hand,[31] vv. 1–3 might be derived from a source. The wording of the verses contains nothing typically Lucan. But their substance seems even to Haenchen so questionable that in this case he agrees with the Tübingen school and lets Luke succumb to an unreliable tradition;[32] this opinion is not quite intelligible in view of his treatment of the scene in Jerusalem.

[31] See the commentaries.
[32] Pp. 425ff./420ff.

Timothy is the child of a mixed marriage. Therefore according to Jewish law Timothy was a Jew.[33] Luke states that Paul circumcised him because of the Jews in those places; they all knew that his father was a Gentile and therefore—evidently this is how Luke imagines the situation—they would have made difficulties for Paul in his missionary work. Of course, if Paul always begins it in the synagogues he can hardly have an uncircumcised Jew as his colleague![34] But we saw that it was Luke's interpretation which made Paul's missionary activity begin in the synagogues. Then it is natural to attribute the account of Timothy's circumcision to this interpretation, which is intended to furnish at every point the evidence so important for Luke, namely that Christianity is a variety of Judaism. At any rate, one thing seems certain: for the sake of his mission, as Luke's account implies, Paul had hardly any need to have Timothy circumcised. He was not a missionary to the Jews.

But what would the church in Jerusalem say if Paul had been accompanied on his mission by an uncircumcised Jew as his closest fellow worker? That would have given all possible support to the charge that Paul was enticing Jews to abandon the Law.[35] The uncircumcised Jew Timothy could have become no small embarrassment to Paul's relationship to the Jewish Christians in Jerusalem, who in view of the unity of Christendom had to take responsibility in the eyes of the Jewish authorities for what Paul did. But Paul had always endeavoured earnestly and in harmony with the Jerusalem church to avoid any such embarrassment, so as neither to subject them to Stephen's fate nor to force them to hold themselves aloof from the Gentile Christians. In view of this it can well be supposed that he had Timothy circumcised.

This must not be contrasted with Gal. 2.3. Titus, who according to this passage in the letter to Galatians was not circumcised, was a Gentile, as Paul adds explicitly (for in the case of a Jew by birth the problem would have presented itself in a different way).

---

[33] Billerbeck II, p. 741. In view of the fact that Timothy was the child of an illegal mixed marriage and uncircumcised, the statements in II Tim. 1.5; 3.15 turn out to be pious legends. Or was the liberal attitude of Hellenistic Jewry so pronounced that illegal conduct of this kind could be compatible with well-known piety?

[34] I do not understand how at the same time Timothy's circumcision can be disputed and Paul's approach to the synagogues can be asserted.

[35] O. Bauernfeind, *Die Apostelgeschichte*, p. 204.

Similarly the remark in Gal. 5.3[36] is made to Gentiles, to whom circumcision could only mean the acceptance of the Law as a religious duty. On the other hand, for the Jew circumcision was first of all admission into the Jewish national community, and for many Jews it was never more than this; for Jewish Christians it remained just this. It was in this sense that Paul recognized the observance of the Law by the Jewish Christians[37] and for prudent and practical reasons relinquished the mission to the Jews which disregarded the Law. But since he did so, it is hard to see why he ought not for the same reasons to circumcise the Jewish-Christian Timothy as well. In that case Luke's account would be correct in that Paul circumcised Timothy because of the Jews, though it was, in fact, not because of the Jews who were the objects of his mission, but because of the hostile Jewry in Jerusalem,[38] to whom no unnecessary and avoidable pretext for taking action against the Christians should be provided.

All this need not prove that Paul actually circumcised Timothy. It only indicates a simple explanation of the reason for a circumcision of this kind, one which was, in fact, really necessary if Timothy was actually uncircumcised. If, therefore, the other details appear to inspire confidence in the critics, nothing prevents us from assuming that Timothy really was circumcised by Paul. In that case this assumption enables us to put aside the difficult task of finding an explanation for the appearance of the unhistorical legend about Timothy's circumcision. For that Luke invented the whole story out of his own head conflicts completely with his literary method.[39]

[36] 'I testify again to every man who receives circumsion that he is bound to keep the whole Law.'

[37] 'Though he had completely abolished the old conditions (of the Law), still for the Jews he had only abolished them as *establishing merit*. He never dreamed of dispensing with them as the given customary law for Jews. Hence in general he lived "as without the Law" but also under certain circumstances as under the Law' (A. von Harnack, *The Date of the Acts and the Synoptic Gospels*, ET [New Testament Studies 4], 1911, p. 55).

[38] Of course, it must also immediately provoke the anger of the Jews in Paul's missionary area if he had surrounded himself with uncircumcised Jews. It was the former who first notified the authorities in Jerusalem. Thus Paul himself would have come to experience the immediate effect of what he was doing. The reason given in 16.3 for Timothy's circumcision might have stood in a source in this sense. διὰ τοὺς 'Ιουδαίους does not necessarily mean: to facilitate the mission to the Jews; it can mean instead: in order to avoid unnecessary difficulties with the Jews (in the mission to the Gentiles).

[39] Of course, Luke could make good use of this account. For it demonstrated what close contact Paul and the Gentile Christians maintained with Judaism.

The other statement belonging to this context occurs in Acts 18.18: Paul was sailing to Syria κειράμενος ἐν Κεγχρεαῖς τὴν κεφαλήν. εἶχεν γὰρ εὐχήν. This remark is unlikely to apply to Aquila, who is accompanying Paul; it applies instead to the apostle himself, as the commentators with few exceptions assume.[40] Evidently a Nazirite vow is in mind.[41] But for that purpose the hair is allowed to *grow*, it is not cut. The release from a vow of this kind had to take place in Jerusalem. There is no evidence for the fact that it was permitted to cut off one's hair abroad beforehand.[42] The Jew coming from abroad had to live for at least thirty days in Judea before he could undertake the ceremonies in the Temple which released him.[43] Paul would therefore have had to spend at least a month in Jerusalem. But there are serious doubts more generally about the journey to Jerusalem mentioned here.[44] Consequently Luke's whole statement is hardly intelligible by itself. It is possible that it goes back to some piece of information which Luke is using. But it tells us nothing which would enable us to understand it. If Paul had really travelled to Jerusalem, he might have done in anticipation as a preventive what the Jewish Christians suggested to him on his last arrival in Jerusalem. But such a hypothesis remains pure speculation and is, moreover, hardly likely.

It is a more natural conjecture that Luke framed at least the vow in 18.18—even if not necessarily the whole journey—on the model of the scene in Acts 21.15–26 in order to make the same point which he adds to the later account by interpretation, namely what a law-abiding Christian Paul had been after all.

It is also not impossible that in addition to the good source of Paul's last stay in Jerusalem Luke possessed a very bad tradition of the same event which, perhaps even without noticing that it was a duplicate, he incorporated into Paul's Syrian journey. We may feel some confidence in the account of this journey to Syria, whilst it is inexplicable why Paul goes from Ephesus to Antioch via Caesarea.[45]

[40] For example, E. Preuschen.
[41] Cf. Acts 18.18 with 21.23f.
[42] Billerbeck II, p. 749.
[43] *Ibid.*
[44] Haenchen, pp. 489f/483f.
[45] *Ibid.*

VI

THE 'APOSTOLIC DECREE'

THE treatment of the problem of the 'Apostolic Decree' by Haenchen[1] is so excellent that we can deal with this matter briefly. The four regulations in the decree come from the Holiness Code of the Old Testament and are found there in the same order[2] as in Acts 15.29 and 21.25:[3] to abstain from what has been sacrificed to idols,[4] from blood, from what has been strangled[5] and from unchastity[6] (Lev. 17f.).[7] These regulations are enjoined not only upon the Jews but also upon pagans living in their land: Lev. 17.8, 12, 13; 18.26. For their infringement defiles the whole land. On the other hand, when the pagans observed them it was possible for Jews and pagans to live together. Thus these regulations served not to cut the Jewish population off from foreigners but to keep the promised land holy, and thereby to enable an existence according to the Law to be lived there. They remained valid for dwellers in Palestine up to the rabbinic period[8] and were doubtless recognized as such also by the God-fearers in the Diaspora,[9] at times supplemented by the law of the sabbath, also binding on non-Jews, and by other regulations (prohibition of pork, etc.).

---

[1] Pp. 415–19/410–14; cf. E. Haenchen in *Judentum, Urchristentum, Kirche* (Festschrift für J. Jeremias, BZNW 26), 1960, pp. 160ff.

[2] We are disregarding the undoubtedly later 'Western' wording of the 'Apostolic Decree'. Cf. W. G. Kümmel, 'Die älteste Form des Apostelrekrets' (in *Spiritus et Veritas*, 1953, pp. 83–98).

[3] Cf. H. Waitz, 'Das Problem des sogenannten Apostelrekrets', ZKG 55, 1936, pp. 228f.

[4] The prohibition of eating meat sacrificed to idols, including particularly the sacrifices in pagan temples.

[5] Meat not slaughtered according to the Jewish ritual.

[6] πορνεία here denotes the consanguineous marriages forbidden in Lev. 18.6–18; Billerbeck II, pp. 729f. Kümmel holds another view in 'Die älteste Form des Apostelrekrets'.

[7] The first three regulations do not mean at all the same thing as Lietzmann (*Kleine Schriften* II, pp. 292ff.) supposes. A glance at Lev. 17f. refutes this conception.

[8] Billerbeck II, pp. 721ff.

[9] For obvious reasons (see Billerbeck II, pp. 716f.) the rabbinic writings only rarely mention the σεβόμενοι. So we depend mainly on the New Testament for information about them. Cf. also Josephus, *c. Apion.* 2.10, 39. Cf. also Schoeps, *Paulus*, pp. 232ff.; see above, pp. 61f.

They form, too, the matrix of the seven so-called Noachic precepts compiled by the rabbinic scholars as God's ordinances binding on *all* people, but hardly likely to have had practical significance.[10]

The regulations of the 'Apostolic Decree' are therefore Mosaic rules for the Gentiles. This was known to Luke, as Acts 15.20f. shows. Consequently in the framework of his presentation of the facts this decree bears witness to the concord between (Gentile) Christianity and Judaism which Luke always emphasizes.[11] What value as history must we assign to it?

That this decree was decided at the 'Apostolic Council' is plainly disproved by Gal. 2.6.[12]

Most commentators today assume that it originated in the period *after* the scene in Antioch described by Paul (Gal. 2.11ff.) and was recommended by the Jewish Christians to the Gentile Christians in order to make table-fellowship possible between them.[13] This thesis is based on Acts 21.25. Here, so the argument runs, the 'Apostolic Decree' is introduced as something unknown to Paul, although Paul himself is, in fact, supposed to have taken it from Jerusalem to Antioch (Acts 15.22ff.) and into his mission area (Acts 16.4). Hence we have in 21.25 an account from a source which Luke has not reconciled with the rest of his story. This source knows that the Apostolic Decree originated in Jerusalem and lets Paul be informed of it here for the first time. This explanation agrees with the fact that Paul shows no knowledge in any of his letters of the regulations contained in these instructions, but allows Gentile Christians to eat meat sacrificed to idols contrary to these regulations (I Cor. 8-10).[14]

[10] Billerbeck II, p. 722; III, pp. 36ff.
[11] Haenchen, pp. 416f./411f.
[12] A different view is held, for example, by Lyder Brun, 'Apostelkoncil und Aposteldekret', in *Paulus und die Urgemeinde*, 1921; A. S. Geyser in *Studia Paulina*, pp. 124ff.
[13] The long list of scholars (in Haenchen, pp. 415/410; cf. Cullmann, *Peter*, pp. 50ff.) holding this point of view could be extended. An astonishing consensus of opinion has developed in this; it is especially astonishing in view of its slender exegetical foundation. Cf. Hahn, *Mission*, pp. 83f.
[14] R. Bultmann ('Zur Frage nach den Quellen der Apostelgeschichte', in *New Testament Essays*, Studies in memory of T. W. Manson, 1959, pp. 71ff.) in a discussion with Haenchen and following W. Bousset (*ZNW* 14, 1913, pp. 156-162) goes farther when he conjectures that in Acts 15 a written source was used 'which told of a conference of which this decree was the outcome' (p. 73). Luke is said to have been the first to introduce Paul and Barnabas to this source. This is rightly rejected by Haenchen (see p. 97, n. 1), pp. 160ff.

But already F. Overbeck[15] and H. J. Holtzmann[16] took a more correct view; Haenchen,[16a] too, is right in insisting with them that it was not a source but Luke who quotes the 'Apostolic Decree' in Acts 21.25. His intention is not to let *Paul* be told about something new, but to inform the *readers* what is the position with regard to the Gentile Christians, after they had heard that Jewish Christians ought to observe the Law in its entirety. It was important for Luke to impress information of this kind repeatedly on his reader; for the fact of the 'Apostolic Decree' certainly displayed the 'Judaizing' bias of the Gentile Christians—that is, really Luke's own bias. We cannot credit even an author who writes with such bold strokes as Luke does with letting Paul be told twice for the first time about the 'Apostolic Decree'. Thus we do not, in fact, learn from Luke at all where the decree originated, since in any case it cannot have been at the 'Apostolic Council'.

Haenchen[17] assumes that it was recognized in Luke's time, perhaps attributed to the apostles already before his time and fitted by him into the history in the way we know.

Now it is, in fact, correct that the Christians continued to forbid consanguineous marriages (πορνεία); it corresponds, indeed, essentially also to Roman law.[18] Moreover, a strong repugnance to eating meat offered to idols can be confirmed for the second century: Justin (*Dial.* 34.8; 35.1); Rev. 2.14, 20; Irenaeus (*Haer.* I 6.3; 24.5; 26.3; 28.2) and Tertullian (*Haer.* 33). But these passages, which can be multiplied, leave us in no doubt that it is always the struggle with libertarian Gnosis which brings home to the Christians of the Church the need to prohibit meat sacrificed to idols.

Finally, Minucius Felix (9.5), Eusebius (*Eccl. Hist.* V 1.26) and Tertullian (*Apol.* 9.13) defend themselves against the stereotyped accusation[19] that they murder and consume children by pointing with equal regularity to the contents of the 'Apostolic Decree',

---

[15] *Kurze Erklärung der Apostelgeschichte*, by W. M. L. de Wette, Leipzig, 1870⁴, pp. 379f., 383f.
[16] P. 132. Cf. also A. Loisy, *Les Actes des Apôtres*, Paris, 1920, pp. 799f.
[16a] Pp. 417/412; 547/541; see also Dibelius, *Acts*, p. 99.
[17] Pp. 417f./412f.; cf. H. Conzelmann in *RGG*³ III, col. 136f.: 'In post-apostolic times we find it in force generally.'
[18] Cf. H. Baltensweiler, 'Die Ehebruchsklauseln bei Matthäus', TZ 15, 1959, pp. 350f.; *id.*, 'Erwägungen zu I Thess. 4.3–8', TZ 19, 1963, pp. 7f.
[19] Cf. also K. Rudolph, *Die Mandäer* I (FRLANT 74), 1960, p. 39 n. 6.

which forbids them even to partake of blood and of meat unless slaughtered according to the Jewish ritual. Therefore, at any rate in times of persecution, they will have behaved in accordance with this decree.

Hence the Christians in the second century, too, attached importance for very different reasons, due to the circumstances of their own time, to the conduct recommended by the 'Apostolic Decree'; but they did not do so in order to make it possible for Jewish Christians and Gentile Christians to live together. So we cannot conclude that the 'Apostolic Decree' was observed up till this period. It was not the Jewish-Christian demands of the so-called 'Apostolic Decree' which induced Christians not to eat meat offered to idols, or strangled flesh or blood, and to refrain from consanguineous marriages, nor was it, of course, the section of Lev. 17f. itself; but it was the struggle against Gnosis in one place, resistance to pagan accusations in another, the observance of the laws of the State in a third. It is accidental that these individual and occasional customs, which were independent of each other, should be paralleled by the summary contents of the 'Apostolic Decree', and the circumstances of the second century do not help in elucidating the origin of this decree, even if a connexion were brought about incidentally in the second century between the behaviour of the Church and this decree made known by Luke.

Thus we remain dependent on conjectures. One of the improbable conjectures is to suppose that the four requirements were issued somewhere in order to make possible table-fellowship between Jewish and Gentile Christians. Those four rules make sense if they are intended to preserve the holiness of Palestine. They have a meaning, too, as a matrix of the observances recommended to a God-fearer. But as a basis for table-fellowship in particular they were inappropriate.[20] They would not even have guaranteed that forbidden meat, e.g. pork, was not served, or that none of the wine had come from a libation. Moreover, Lev. 17f. plays no part in the rabbinic rules for table-fellowship with the Gentiles.[21] For the fellowship at the Lord's supper, at which it was not customary to partake of meat, the decree was completely

---

[20] Cf. K. T. Schäfer, article 'Aposteldekret' in *RAC* I, cols. 556f.

[21] Billerbeck IV 1, pp. 374ff. Even Luke could hardly have supposed that there was a relationship between the 'Apostolic Decree' and table-fellowship; a glance at Acts 10.15; 11.3 shows this.

unsuitable. And yet the celebration of the Lord's Supper in common undoubtedly set the pattern for more general table-fellowship between Jewish and Gentile Christians.

Perhaps the regulations of the Apostolic Decree never had their *Sitz im Leben* in the Christian Church,[22] but, since Luke is hardly likely to have quoted them directly from Lev. 17f., they may have reached him from circles in Diaspora Jewry.[23] In these they could and might have been recognized as minimum rules for the uncircumcised God-fearing Gentiles who yet lived in association with the synagogue. For undoubtedly when Jews and pagans shared in the life of the synagogue, provisions for purity were necessary, similar to those to which Lev. 17f. bears witness for the life together of both peoples on the soil of Palestine.[24] We have seen what good use Luke was able to make of this decree.

It might, of course, also be that a way of life, developed originally by the so-called σεβόμενοι, was gradually accepted, too, by the Gentile Christians, of whom many had, in fact, stood in a similar relationship to Judaism.[25] But that can only have occurred to a limited extent, for apart from the reports in Acts no traces of the existence of the 'Apostolic Decree' can be found in early Christian literature.[26] Nor do the Pauline letters know anything of

---

[22] G. Strecker, 'Christentum', p. 463, and *RGG* IV³, cols. 1500f., also expresses basic doubts about the historicity of the 'Apostolic Decree'.

[23] The fact that some of the rules out of Lev. 17f. are in conformity with the behaviour of the sub-apostolic Church may have attracted Luke's attention and prompted him to declare the four rules to be an apostolic decree; for in this way he could give an example as evidence for the Jewishness of the authentic apostolic tradition, obligatory for all time.

[24] Cf. K. T. Schäfer in *RAC* I, cols. 536f., who considers it possible that the stipulations of the 'Apostolic Decree' 'transfer to Gentile Christians regulations which in the synagogue community were intended for the so-called "God-fearing" Gentiles (the seven "Noachic precepts" compiled later by the Rabbis and regarded as binding on all mankind contain, in fact, the substance of these stipulations)'. Schoeps, too, points to the connexion between the 'Noachic precepts' and the rules of the 'Apostolic Decree' (*Paulus*, pp. 60, 237; *Theologie*, pp. 259f.). The closer this connexion is—rightly—regarded to be, the less grounds are there for the assertion that the *Sitz im Leben* of the 'Apostolic Decree' was in the early *Christian* communities.

In conclusion I refer to E. Dinkler, 'Zum Problem der Ethik bei Paulus', *ZTK* 49, 1952, pp. 195f., and to the literature given there on p. 195, n. 5; this demonstrates how great an influence Lev. 17-20 had altogether on Hellenistic Christendom; it was, in fact, exerted, so we must assume, by the adoption of the synagogical instructions for proselytes and God-fearers based on the Holiness Code of Lev. 17-20.

[25] Holtzmann, *Die Apostelgeschichte*, p. 98; cf. G. Stählin, *Die Apostelgeschichte* (NTD 5), 1962, p. 105.

[26] Lietzmann conjectures (*Kleine Schriften* II, pp. 297f.) that it was known in Corinth in a shortened form and was made by the Corinthians the subject of an

the practice conjectured by H. J. Holtzmann, which is surely the harder to imagine the later it occurred. It is quite impossible that the 'Apostolic Decree' as a *Jewish-Christian requirement* could still have become established in the Gentile-Christian churches after the death of Paul—for in his time the four rules were unknown to the churches. That could have happened only as an exceptional case in a place where Jewish Christians formed the majority, therefore hardly anywhere else but in Jerusalem. But there is no indication, not even from Luke, that in fact it did happen there.

Whatever may be the position in detail, one way or another the 'decree' has no great significance for the problem of the relationship between the Jewish and the Gentile Christians; for after all that has been said, it is not only open to doubt whether it originated in primitive Christianity but also whether it was ever recognized there at all.

---

inquiry in their letters answered by Paul in I Cor. But this inquiry had another background: cf. Schmithals, *Die Gnosis in Korinth*, pp. 183ff.

VII

JUDAIZERS?

WE must sum up the result of our inquiry. Paul and the Jerusalem Christians were always concerned to preserve the unity of the Church.[1] That this was no simple task was not in the first place due to theological differences which may have existed between Paul and James,[2] but to the need and the difficulty for the Jewish-Christian church to preserve the possibility of existence in Jerusalem or Palestine. This need required the Gentile Christians, in view of their propaganda amongst the Jews, to take certain measures of considerate regard for the Jewish Christians. These measures Paul guaranteed and observed by relinquishing the mission to the Jews which the Jerusalem Christians took upon themselves. In this way it was possible to assure the unity of the Church until beyond the year 60—and this means practically up to the Jewish revolt, which in any case created fresh circumstances—nevertheless, the Jewish Christians in Jerusalem did not remain completely exempt from bloody persecutions.

---

[1] So also Schoeps, *Paulus*, pp. 57–64, who comes to the conclusion that Paul and the Jerusalem Christians 'worked together and not against each other'. 'The conception of the Tübingen school that there was a deep gulf between Paul on the one hand, James and Peter on the other, when re-examined impartially, does not hold water' (pp. 62f.).

[2] Our inquiry has to a large extent left on one side the theological questions in the narrower sense. This was not done from lack of interest in these problems, but was due to the texts which tell us a variety of things about Paul's relationship to James, but exclude theological differences in particular from their range of vision. It is just those theological differences which have, in fact, up till now been considered by scholars to be the real source of tension between Jewish and Gentile Christians. Now, I am far from casting the least doubts on the theological variety of primitive Christianity. But in any case theological differences between Paul and James were not significant enough to separate the churches; cf. Cullmann, *Peter*, pp. 52ff.

It might be asked: What is the position of Christology? The answer is that even Paul did not possess a Christology in our sense at all. For the whole of primitive Christianity Christology is something which is variable (H. Braun, 'Der Sinn der neutestamentlichen Christologie', *ZTK* 54, 1957, pp. 341ff.). And what about the Law? We have already spoken of it incidentally. Of course, the primitive church in Jerusalem did not abide by the concepts of the Pauline doctrine of justification any more than the whole synoptic tradition did. But like Paul it sought salvation in

87   Paul and James

Now, the relationship of Paul to the primitive church in Jerusalem is, in fact, only a special case of the whole attitude towards each other of the Gentile and the Jewish Christians. But this special case is unquestionably characteristic of their whole relationship, especially as the sphere of influence of Paul on the one hand and of James and/or Peter[3] on the other included a considerable, if not the predominant, part of the Christendom of that period. We do not wish to imply that all movements in primitive Christianity can

---

Christ and not in the Law. Paul's doctrine of justification is anti-Pharisaic and at no point is it developed in opposition to Jewish Christianity. A wrong historical understanding of the letter to the Galatians has caused much perplexity in this respect.

Did decisive differences exist between Paul and the Jerusalem Christians in their attitude to the historical Jesus? In view of the fact that Paul practically ignored the historical Jesus this seems to have been the case. So far as I know, no one has yet given consideration to the fact that the Jerusalem Christians might be equally ignorant. Yet even in this matter we must be on our guard against too definite a judgement. In primitive Christianity Paul's attitude to the historical Jesus seems to have been by no means peculiar, but was much more likely to have been typical (see Schmithals, 'Paulus und der historische Jesus', *ZNW* 53, 1962, pp. 145ff.). Paul hardly possesses any knowledge at all of the historical tradition concerning Jesus. In view of this fact and of the relatively close connexion existing between Paul and Jerusalem in regard to their common missionary activity, it does not seem exactly probable that the attitude of the Jerusalem church to the historical Jesus differed basically from that of Paul. On the other hand, Paul never calls in question the historical Jesus, nor does he question the theology or the gospel founded on him; on the contrary, he regrets having no saying of the Lord to put forward. This fact, too, excludes remarkable differences between Paul and the Jerusalem church in their attitude to the historical Jesus.

In short: since the time of the Tübingen school our scholars have taken for granted as the presupposition of all their studies of primitive Christianity that there were weighty theological antagonisms between Paul and James. This foregone conclusion, accepted as a matter of course, is in urgent need of re-examination.

[3] Not infrequently tensions are thought to exist between Peter and James, or between the Jewish-Christian circles which they each represent; cf., for example, Cullmann, *Peter*, pp. 48, 52ff.; see also p. 114, n. 35 below. Our examination of the texts in question has produced nothing which would lead to this supposition. On the contrary the events in Antioch recorded by Paul in Gal. 2.11ff. bear witness to the fundamental community of interest between Peter and James as regards their actions; for Peter evidently defers to the wishes of the Jerusalem Christians without reservations. In any case Paul regards the Jewish Christians of Palestine as a unity represented by Peter and James. Naturally theological differences may have existed amongst the Judean Jewish Christians also, but we know nothing about them because we know hardly anything reliable at all about the theology of the Jewish Christians in Judea in the period before 70. That the later Ebionites seek support in James and not in Peter is an indication that they developed out of the early Palestinian Jewish Christianity of which James was the head in Jerusalem. That Peter, on the other hand, was regarded as the leading figure amongst the Jewish Christians in the Diaspora is shown, for instance, by the first letter of Peter (cf. p. 51 above). No deductions can be drawn from these facts with regard to any strained relations between James and Peter, any more than to the supposition that James shows a stronger bias towards Judaism than Peter, which is, of course, possible.

be fitted into the basically quite simple picture which we have drawn. Even if we leave Gnosticism out of account, there remain elements which at first sight are incompatible with this picture. If we examine them more closely, there are, in fact, fewer of them than modern scholars are inclined to assume, even those who would place themselves in opposition to F. C. Baur.[4]

Where do we find elements of this kind?

Apart from the Gnostics we know by name no branch of primitive Christendom which withdrew itself from the Christian fellowship characterized by the figures of Paul and James and by their agreement to differ. The discussion between Paul on the one hand and Peter and Barnabas on the other took place *within* this fellowship and never called it in question. Only a wrong exegesis occasionally made Apollos into an opponent of Paul, who speaks of him only as a fellow worker.

Undoubtedly the beginnings of Jewish Christianity did not remain without influence on the later Jewish-Christian sects about whom we have sparse information from the early Church Fathers, from Gospel fragments, the Clementine literature and a few other sources. There is evidence for this already in the fact that James is the 'hero' of these circles.[5] But these sects, starting from the line taken by the main body of the Church and going all the way to that of the Gnostics, show so great a variety and at the same time such numerous obviously foreign influences that it is impossible to gain from their traditions authentic material for the attitude of the primitive Jewish-Christian church.[6] Therefore Schoeps in his book on this subject confines himself rightly to Jewish Christianity after 70.[7] What we have established does not mean that Jewish Christianity must have begun to develop into a heresy only after 70; but it does mean that we cannot deduce

[4] Schoeps, too (*Paulus*, pp. 57–64), greatly overestimates the significance of the intransigent Judaizers when the attitude of James to Peter is correctly assessed.

He lets himself be led astray by Acts 15, so as to make James and Peter the authoritative leaders of a central group which has Paul on its left, whilst on its right 'the conservative, Pharisaic primitive Christians in Jerusalem', the real Judaizers, are said to hold a strong position (p. 59).

[5] Cf. also Schoeps, *Urgemeinde*, p. 8; see below.

[6] Cf. K. Rudolph, *Die Mandäer* I, p. 245.

[7] *Theologie und Geschichte des Judenchristentums*, for example p. 7. Unfortunately he does not keep to this praiseworthy rule consistently enough, and his critics have been justified in blaming him for this. His defence against these critics in *Urgemeinde*, pp. 3–29, only justifies them still further in this respect.

from the sources concerning Jewish Christianity, rejected by the Church as heretical, any evidence for a heretical Jewish Christianity existing before the year 70, much less still any reliable information about the nature of such a heresy.[8]

When seeking an answer to our question we must naturally leave out of account those opponents whom Paul attacks as intruders into his churches. In order to modify and tone down F. C. Baur's historical sketch it has today become customary to assign these opponents, or perhaps groups of them, to some kind of Jewish-Christian circles in Palestine with an ultra-Jacobean bias,[9] who had not indeed been sent directly by James, but who had a certain right to appeal to him; usually these groups in addition to an extreme Judaizing bias have also more or less strong Hellenistic or Gnosticizing trends attributed to them.[10] But it is precarious to construct out of isolated sections of Paul's letters the most diverse heresies of which we hear nothing either before or afterwards. It is still more precarious to harmonize conflicting hypotheses by means of the more than questionable information, not supported by any text, that these people had indeed actually but wrongly appealed to James (and Peter). It seems to me certain that these opponents were Jewish or Jewish-Christian Gnostics. As such they have little or nothing to do with the primitive Jewish-Christian church.

There remain as possible evidence for a heretical form of Christianity in the primitive Christian period—always leaving Gnosticism[11] out of account—one remark each from Paul and in the Acts and some sections of the synoptic tradition. These are always concerned with possible indications of an extreme Jewish Christianity. I am not aware of any traces preserved from the period before 70 of a *Gentile* Christianity within the Church, which in a radical ultra-Pauline spirit required the Jews to become antinomian and hence to abandon the Jerusalem agreement.[12]

---

[8] Cf., for example, the opinion of G. Strecker about the oldest source of this literature: 'It cannot, of course, be proved that the author of the *Kerygmata Petrou* used traditional material going back in any form to the primitive Church' (p. 196; cf. p. 253).

[9] Cf. Kümmel in *RGG*³ III, col. 969; Schoeps, *Urgemeinde*, p. 7.

[10] H. Köster in *RGG*³ III, col. 18.

[11] Nor are we concerning ourselves here with the problems touched upon in note 71, paragraph 2, on p. 34.

[12] We may leave out of account here the circle of Stephen which was broken up in early days.

Unfortunately we have no information of any kind from the very area which seems to have been the real home of the early Christian heresies, namely eastern Syria and Mesopotamia. If we did possess such information it would probably have, in fact, no interest as regards our inquiry. So far as we can see, a Gnostic rather than a Judaistic Jewish Christianity was at home there.

The remark made by Paul which we have mentioned occurs in Gal. 2.4f.: διὰ δὲ τοὺς παρεισάκτους ψευδαδέλφους, οἵτινες παρεισῆλθον κατασκοπῆσαι τὴν ἐλευθερίαν ἡμῶν ἣν ἔχομεν ἐν Χριστῷ Ἰησοῦ, ἵνα ἡμᾶς καταδουλώσουσιν. οἷς οὐδὲ πρὸς ὥραν εἴξαμεν τῇ ὑποταγῇ, ἵνα ἡ ἀλήθεια τοῦ εὐαγγελίου διαμείνῃ πρὸς ὑμᾶς.

This sentence contains many problems. We are interested only in the question as to the identity of the false brethren mentioned here. They crept into the deliberations, hence they do not really belong to the assembled circle of the brethren; they wish to spy out the Christians' freedom from the Law, or even to carry out an official inspection;[13] evidently their first object is to subject Paul anew to the Law. These people may have been Jews officially commissioned to investigate the attitude of the Christian church.

There can surely be no doubt that the Christian Church was under official observation, especially after the persecution of Stephen's circle. The Jews had to remain informed about the position of the Christians regarding the Law, and the 'false brethren'[14] were after all able to present themselves as people of some importance. This would chime in with the conjecture expressed above (p. 52) that an official record was made for the

---

[13] See Schlier, *Galater*, p. 39.

[14] It ought not to be said that Paul could not have called unbaptized Jews ψευδάδελφοι. To call a fellow member of one's religion 'brother' comes from Judaism, and it is only natural that the emissaries of the Jerusalem Jews introduced themselves to the Apostolic Council as 'brethren', especially if they wished to test the correctness of the Christians' Judaism. In Paul's view these brethren are naturally 'false brethren'. Cf. H. von Soden in *TWNT* I, 145f.

In any case no difference is made by the fact established by K. Wegenast, *Verständnis der Tradition*, p. 47 n. 1, that Paul does not call Jews brothers, but brothers according to the flesh. He certainly gives them the latter name, but the former one fits, too, and particularly in Gal. 2.4 as well, where he speaks explicitly of *false* brethren. After all, he could not speak of 'false brethren according to the flesh'!

I think A. S. Geyser is altogether on the wrong track when he proposes (*Studia Paulina*, pp. 124ff.) that Gal. 2.4f. should be put in brackets and that it describes not the former situation in Jerusalem but the present one in Galatia. At the most, serious consideration might be given by some scholars to the possibility of applying Gal. 2.4f. to the events in Antioch before the 'Apostolic Council'; yet this, too, appears to me to be highly improbable. In this connexion reference must also be made to D. Warner, 'Galatians 2.3–8 as an Interpolation', *ExpT* 62, 1950–1, p. 380.

Jewish authorities of the arrangements agreed at the 'Apostolic Council'. If that is so, then the 'we' in ἔχομεν and the ἡμᾶς *might* include Paul and the 'pillars', and so the whole of Christendom.

It is, indeed, universally assumed that these false brethren were members of a Judaistic group of the primitive Church, even if of an extreme one, but yet were baptized Christians.[15] The weightiness with which they presented themselves and were enabled to obtain a hearing certainly conflicts with the view that they were only a small separate Christian group. Besides we never meet with such people elsewhere in Paul's writings. He always describes the primitive community as a united body and his opponents in Jerusalem are elsewhere always the Jews. The παρ ... in παρεισάκτους and in παρεισῆλθον indicates intruders with emphasis on their having no business to be in the assembly of the Christian Church; that applies to Jews, but hardly to any kind of Jewish Christians in Jerusalem.

On the other hand, it is, of course, quite understandable if there appeared amongst groups of the Jerusalem Christians who were exposed to danger, especially when they remembered the persecutions, a greater readiness for a life in obedience to the Law, in order in this way to escape from such a threat. Evidently Paul is thinking of such tendencies in Gal. 5.11; 6.12f. and there is no reason against seeking in this early period the beginnings of the anti-Paulinism of heretical Ebionitism. I do not dare to make a definite decision on this question, although the first conjecture seems to me to be by far the most probable.[16]

The statements made in Acts 15.5, 24 hardly facilitate this decision. Luke's description of the 'Apostolic Council' has no historical value. There is certainly no historical basis for the fact that the demand for circumcision by certain Christian circles was *ever* the occasion for the meeting in Jerusalem. Moreover, according to Luke's account missionary work amongst the Gentiles had

---

[15] Schoeps, *Urgemeinde*, p. 7.
[16] The question what the 'false brethren secretly brought in' demanded of Paul, and what Paul had then refused to give 'that the truth of the gospel might be preserved for you' (2.5) cannot be answered with regard to either of the possible meanings just considered, for Paul says nothing about it. Was the circumcision of all Gentile Christians demanded? Should the Gentile Christians receive the status of proselytes? Was a minimum observance of the Law expected of the Gentile Christians, as was undoubtedly the case for the God-fearers? Were Paul and the Jewish-Christian missionaries amongst the Gentiles required to live according to the Law in their personal lives? We do not know.

long been going on at the time of the 'Apostolic Council', and was, moreover, sanctioned by the Jerusalem Christians (Acts 10f.); hence the demand for circumcision assigned by Luke as the cause of the 'Council' could come only from a minority in the church. In that case it was most natural to think of τινὲς τῶν ἀπὸ τῆς αἱρέσεως τῶν Φαρισαίων πεπιστευκότες. We can scarcely find historical reminiscences in this statement. In any case Acts 15.5, 24 is no more able than Gal. 2.4f. to *prove* the existence of a strictly Judaistic and ultra-Jacobean group of Jewish Christians in Jerusalem.[17]

Some passages in the synoptic tradition are more instructive regarding our question. It is obvious that the synoptic tradition as a whole is not favourably disposed to the Law, but constantly defends the Christians' open-minded attitude to it, partly in the form of controversies with the Pharisees.[18] On this point evidently Palestinian and Hellenist traditions meet.[19] The observance of certain legal customs imposed by membership of Palestinian Jewry, which is noticeable,[19a] too, in the synoptic tradition, does not restrict this verdict. But perhaps Matt. 5.17-20 (cf. Luke 16.17) makes an exception.

Verse 17 might originally have been an independent logion. If it is understood in the sense of Rom. 10.4 (Christ is the end of the Law), it asserts nothing in favour of a Judaistic legalism. But probably v. 17 was formed by Matthew[20] and as such was in any case not Judaistic, in whatever sense the πληρῶσαι is understood.

---

[17] Still less is it possible to deduce from Gal. 2.11f. with W. G. Kümmel that there was 'an extremely conservative minority in the Jerusalem church' (*RGG*³ VI, col. 1189).

[18] Here Matt. 17.24-27 deserves special attention. This section provides evidence for the fact that in Jewish-Christian circles the Temple tax was indeed paid, but it declares at the same time that in principle Christians are exempt from this payment. It should be made only from tactical considerations, so as not to give any offence. We must not explain it with Schniewind: 'Jesus pays the tax, because the temple is God's sanctuary' (NTD 2, *ad loc.*)—in this cultic sense Christians in particular are exempted from the payment—but the reason given for the payment means in practice: for the sake of peace with the Jews, to avoid persecution, 'the disciples of Jesus pay the Temple tax as free sons, merely in order not to give offence' (G. Bornkamm, 'Matthew', p. 20; similarly G. Barth, 'Matthew's Understanding of the Law', p. 90). Cf. p. 48 n. 28.

[19] '. . . Could men preserve Jesus' critical and polemic words against Jewish legalism without orienting themselves by them? Could a man pass on Jesus' words against counting up reward and against the pride of the legally correct and at the same time impose a condition of legal merit upon the sharing of salvation?' (Bultmann, *Theology* I, p. 54).

[19a] Cf. G. Strecker, 'Christentum', p. 462.

[20] Cf. G. Barth, pp. 66ff.; Strecker, *Gerechtigkeit*, pp. 144f.

Verse 20, too, was probably framed by Matthew as an introduction to the antitheses which follow;[21] at any rate, the verse is not meant to promulgate a particularly extreme legalism, but love as a better righteousness than that of Pharisaic legalism.[22] Thus the saying is critical of the Law.

Verses 18f. contain a common rabbinical axiom[23] with which Mark 13.31 and par. and I *Clem.* 27.5 should be compared. The verses contain nothing specifically Christian. In view of the manner in which Matthew has used these verses which he has taken over we must ask whether v. 17 is intended to be used for the interpretation of the context in which they are found, so that it means: In Christ the Law is fulfilled down to the last iota, or—with J. Schniewind[24]—whether we are meant to use v. 20, which would in that case also govern the sense of v. 17: through Jesus' interpretation of the Law, the ultimate and inviolable sense of the Law is brought out. Of course, that is not their original meaning; but it is in any case the sense given to them by Matthew in the context of his theology, and perhaps it is already the sense to which they owe their being taken over from a Jewish tradition into that of the Church, unless Matthew was the first to appropriate this well-known Jewish axiom and deliberately to give it a Christian meaning, and this is the most natural hypothesis.[25]

Yet possibly they made their way into the synoptic tradition through Q from the traditions of a circle of *Christians* who were loyal to the Law. This is the usual assumption,[26] which is, how-

---

[21] R. Bultmann, *History*, p. 138; Strecker, *Gerechtigkeit*, pp. 151.
[22] Cf. Barth, pp. 79f.
[23] Billerbeck I, pp. 244ff.; G. Barth, p. 65. Both verses may have existed originally apart from each other. Luke 16.17 should be compared with v. 18. On the problem of the tradition see H. Schürmann, *BZ* 4, pp. 238ff.; W. Trilling, *Das wahre Israel*, pp. 138ff. (with the literature); V. Hasler, *Gesetz und Evangelium in der alten Kirche bis Origenes*, 1953, pp. 9ff.
[24] NTD 2, 1937, *ad loc.*; G. Bornkamm, 'Matthew', 24ff.; Strecker, *Gerechtigkeit*, pp. 146f.
[25] Matthew's intention in revising and admitting these sayings is obvious; he is attacking antinomians, as he is doing in Matt. 7.15ff and 24.11ff. as well. What kind of antinomians these were is difficult to decide precisely. Since they are presumably libertinists, the Pauline churches are excluded in any case. Cf. on this question Barth, pp. 159ff. Moreover, if we observe that Matt. 5.17-20 forms an introduction to the antitheses in the Sermon on the Mount which bear a partial resemblance to the doctrine of Marcion, we readily understand the purpose of these verses which draw upon traditional Jewish material, and we shall at the same time be on our guard against deducing from them that Matthew's attitude was that of a Jewish Christian.
[26] Munck, *Paul*, pp. 253f.; Bultmann, *History*, p. 138; G. Bornkamm, 'Matthew',

ever, altogether doubtful, and in view of the peculiar nature of these verses makes them at best represent merely an offshoot of Jewish Christianity, certainly not the majority represented by James. Since these verses contain nothing of a Christian nature, this last interpretation must be considered to be the less probable one.

There is more material about those trends in primitive Christianity which consist in a guarded attitude amongst certain Christian circles towards the Gentile mission. Here, too, it is true to say that taken as a whole the synoptic tradition accepts this mission as a matter of course[27] and defends it aggressively against Judaism. But the stories of the Syrophoenician woman (Mark 7.24–30 and par.) and the centurion of Capernaum (Matt. 8.5–10 and par.) were, after all, evidently handed down in order to meet objections to the Gentile mission by asserting that Jesus, too— even if only in exceptional cases—opened the door into his kingdom to Gentiles.

This certainly by no means proves as yet the existence of rigid Jewish Christians. It is more likely that the stories just mentioned had their *Sitz im Leben* in that period of early Christianity when the Gentile mission was going out from Galilee as well—that is where these stories took place. In that case they provide no evidence for resistance to such a new kind of mission, but only for approval of it. Besides, the story of the Syrophoenician woman, especially in its—possibly older[28]—version in Matthew (15.21–28), shows that the Gentile mission was regarded at first as an exception.

But what about Matt. 10.5f., 23? Both logia are undoubtedly of Christian origin. They can be regarded, as they are by J. Jeremias,[29] as going back to Jesus; they can be imagined as coming into being at the beginning of the Gentile mission in the area of Galilee or Antioch or in the discussion between 'Hebrews' and 'Hellenists' in Jerusalem; or they originated amongst Jewish

---

p. 24; Barth, pp. 64ff.; E. Käsemann in *ZTK* 57, 1960, pp. 165f.; H. Schürmann, *BZ* 4, pp. 238ff., especially pp. 249f.

[27] See in J. Jeremias, *Jesus' Promise to the Nations*, pp. 40ff.
[28] Cf. R. Bultmann, *History*, p. 38.
[29] *Op. cit.*, pp. 19–39.

Christians who did not concur with the agreements of the 'Apostolic Council'; perhaps, too, they were framed by that group which clung loyally to the Law and the possible traces of which we have brought to light.[30]

Yet it seems to me open to question that we hear in these words in one way or another 'the voice of the strictest Jewish Christianity which strenuously resisted a mission beyond the frontiers of Israel'.[31]

Both passages occur within old compilations of rules for Jewish-Christian missionaries. Matt. 10.23 is at the same time in its present form a word of consolation in view of the persecutions.[32] The parousia is close at hand; even if the missionaries have to leave one city after the other in hasty flight, they will not be able to preach in all the cities of Israel before it appears. This saying does not have any kind of mission to the Gentiles in view; such an idea cannot possibly as yet be within the range of its conceptions. Matt. 10.5b–6 is more accurately described as an instruction to Jewish-Christian missionaries to restrict their mission work to the Jews and to pass over Gentiles and Samaritans. Is this saying intended to exclude Gentiles and Samaritans from salvation? That can hardly be! On the contrary, this instruction complies completely with the agreement of the 'Apostolic Council', which gave a precise legal form to a long-established practice, namely that the mission to the Gentiles (and Samaritans) is the concern of the Gentile-Christian church in Antioch; the Palestinian Christians confine themselves to the mission amongst the Jews. We have seen that this limitation was in the interests of the Jewish-Christian church of Palestine and why this was so; the issuing of appropriate instructions to their own missionaries is therefore easy to understand. This in no way involves rejecting the mission to the Gentiles.

Thus in the synoptic tradition, too, there is to be found no

---

[30] Of course, rejection of the Gentile mission need not have been combined with strict legalism—and *vice versa*.

[31] These words are used by E. Käsemann in *ZTK* 57, 1960, p. 167, when reproducing the general view about these passages.

[32] Cf. H. E. Tödt, pp. 60 ff., and most recently E. Bammel, 'Matt. 10.23', *Studia Theologica* 15, 1962, pp. 79ff.; here there is also a short introduction to the problems of the history of the tradition and the literature about it. If Bammel's explanation were right, and the saying had originally nothing at all to do with mission, it drops out of our inquiry completely.

single trace of a strictly legalistic Jewish Christianity which rejected the mission to the Gentiles.[33]

In this connexion we must take note of the fact that the heretical Jewish Christians of the second century appeal to James as the standard of authority in primitive Christianity. But if, as we saw, there existed between Paul and James a relationship expressing a

[33] It is often said that there was in primitive Christianity an anti-Petrine party behind which the adherents of James are then seen to stand. Not infrequently the existence of this party is relied on as an undisputed fact (e.g. E. Bammel in *TZ* 11, 1955, pp. 401-19). Klein, 'Verleugnung', looks for the origin of the denial story to this party which is said to have framed the story of his threefold denial on the basis of Peter's alleged threefold change of position (from leader of the circle of the Twelve, first to apostle, then to one of the στῦλοι in Jerusalem, as a subordinate of James, and finally to one of the missionaries in the Diaspora and independent of James).

Now, Klein is undoubtedly right in saying that the story of the denial cannot originally have been firmly fixed in its present place in the passion story; his treatment of this question is brilliant. Nor can there be any doubt that the narrative as we have it bears a literary character. Nevertheless for various reasons which cannot be set out here in detail, Klein's interpretation of the tradition appears to me to be impossible. To start with, the form in which the change of position is asserted is, in my opinion, not defensible. Nor in any case could even one of these 'changes of position' be a moral disqualification for Peter as a sign of human untrustworthiness and thus give rise to the story of his denial.

Nor do I think that the historicity of a denial by Peter can in any way be called in question. The historical setting of the denial tradition may be indeed in the period between Good Friday and Easter in which Peter—evidently in contrast to other disciples—denied Jesus and the hope which he had aroused. The account of it was handed down, because by means of it a welcome effect of contrast with Peter's later Easter witness was obtained, and this effect was of as much benefit to his witness as the stories of Paul's period as a persecutor benefited his preaching. The intention to disqualify Peter is therefore just as remote from the tradition of the denial as a similar intention with regard to the tradition about Paul as a persecutor. The denial story, like the tradition of Judas's betrayal, which also came into being originally after Easter (see Schmithals, *Apostelamt*, p. 59), soon found its place in the passion story chosen with literary skill. Traces of the historical denial by Peter can also be found in Mark 8.32 and Matt. 14.28-31, passages which may likewise owe their transmission to the contrast with Peter's witness at Easter. This, too, is the only way of explaining why the traditions of the denial were admitted so early into the Gospel writings; for these have by no means a hostile attitude towards Peter.

Consequently the traditions just mentioned contain nothing to support an alleged anti-Petrine party. This is even more true of the remaining traces of this party which Klein enumerates on pp. 324ff. The most important of them, namely the fact that the accounts of the Easter appearances to Peter (and to the other first witnesses!) recede into the background for the benefit of the accounts of the empty tomb, obviously serves the purpose of an objective guarantee of the resurrection evidence and cannot possibly be explained with Klein as due to anti-Petrine resentment. There is, in fact, no evidence of this from the period before 70.

J. Schreiber ('Die Christologie des Markusevangeliums', *ZTK* 58, 1961, pp. 154-83) in his attempt to establish the setting of the Gospel of Mark in the life of early Christianity, an attempt which in itself deserves our praise, comes to the conclusion that Mark is writing his Gospel as the spokesman of Hellenistic Christians whose home was in Galilee in opposition to the Jewish Christians of Judea represented by the figure of Peter; I remain unconvinced by anything said in this argument.

community of interests, then the appeal of the later Judaizers indicates that the Palestinian Jewish Christians who recognized the authority of James took a sectarian course only at a later date. Parallel to this development within Jewish Christianity there is Judaism's complete change of attitude, setting in at the year 70, with regard to proselytism in the Gentile world and the abandonment of the hitherto vigorous missionary activity.[34] The development of a trend towards legalism in the Jewish-Christian groups of Palestine may in that case have had the same cause, the catastrophe of the Jewish war. But that would mean that true Judaism belongs only to the period after 70.[35]

Now I do not expect anyone to agree with this result of our considerations. Nevertheless, the traces of an early non-conforming Jewish Christianity are at best extremely faint in comparison with our traditions as a whole; Bultmann's conjecture,[36] made with Jesus' open-minded attitude to the Law in mind, that 'presumably a retrogression had taken place, so that the old scruples and fidelity to the Law had gradually gained ground, such as was completely the case later with Jewish-Christian sects' does not yet apply to James or to the majority of Jewish Christians before 70,[37] unless the necessary and possibly increasing tactical consideration for the exigencies of their Jewish environment should be designated as a 'return to the Law'. Of course, that opinion is justified without qualification when, for example, the synoptic tradition is compared with Ebionitism.

It is a matter of indifference whether the rise of 'Judaizing' is placed in the years before or in the period after the destruction of

---

[34] Cf. Schoeps, *Paulus*, pp. 232ff.

[35] This is precisely what Munck believes. Cf. 'Jewish Christianity in Post-Apostolic Times' (*NTS* 6, 1960, pp. 103-16). He does indeed at the same time deny any continuity between the Jewish Christianity of Palestine before 70 and the later Ebionitism. Early Jewish Christianity never really survived the Jewish catastrophe of the year 70. Ebionitism is said to have grown out of Gentile Christianity, which in post-apostolic times developed in the direction of a nomistic understanding of the Old Testament. Similarly Munck had already earlier (*Paul*, pp. 87ff.) explained the alleged Judaistic heresy in Galatia by an *ad hoc* misunderstanding amongst the Galatians of Paul's preaching!

I consider all this to be a quite arbitrary theory, which cannot be substantiated exegetically in any discussible manner. Moreover, the disappearance of Jewish Christianity in the year 70 cannot be proved; in fact, it is out of the question in view of the not inconsiderable evidence for Jewish Christianity in Palestine in post-apostolic times and the increasing esteem in which James was held (see pp. 105f.).

[36] *Theology* I, p. 55; cf. Strecker, 'Christentum', p. 462.

[37] See also G. Kittel in *ZNW* 30, 1931, pp. 145-57.

Jerusalem; the history of this Judaizing was without essential significance for the development of the early Church.

On the other hand, it is hardly possible to overestimate the influence of that Jewish Christianity, which under the leadership of Peter shared in the missionary work with Paul at the 'Apostolic Council', if we watch the development of the Church in the first and second centuries. However, in doing so we must certainly take account of the fact that this Jewish Christianity did not consist of an unchangeable unity. In the Palestinian area it was tied to the Law to a presumably increasing extent up to the year 70; parts of this Palestinian Jewish Christianity transformed themselves sooner or later into the above-mentioned 'Judaizing' element. Outside Palestine, on the other hand, this Jewish Christianity bore from the beginning Hellenistic traits (in this matter the concept 'Palestine' must be taken in a very narrow sense and may not be extended without qualification even to Galilee, whilst the concept 'Hellenistic' can scarcely be understood in a sufficiently comprehensive sense).

Indeed, more than this: the exclusively Jewish-Christian nature of this movement in primitive Christianity began to disappear more and more, and first in the West of the Roman Empire. The arrangements made in Jerusalem laid Peter and his circle under a definite obligation to preach Christianity to the Jews, which means, in fact, to preach in the area of the synagogues, and this led necessarily to endeavours to convert the Gentiles to precisely the same extent as that to which the synagogue had brought God-fearers and proselytes under their control. The more closely Gentiles had attached themselves to the synagogue—and it was pointed out on pp. 61f. above that this occurred to a considerable extent—the more thoroughly was Hellenistic Jewish Christianity also permeated by Gentile members.[38] Since already before the year 70 Hellenistic Jewish Christianity probably practised a greater freedom regarding the Law than the synagogue—we need only think of Peter in Antioch—the attractive power of Jewish

---

[38] Cf. Matt. 8.5–13; Mark 7.24–30 par.; Acts 10.1–11.18. This must not be regarded as a breach of the agreements of the 'Apostolic Council'. For not only were proselytes considered as Jews. The question whether Gentiles were allowed to be admitted into the Jewish-Christian churches and under what conditions this might take place was not even a matter dealt with by the Jerusalem agreement. So far as it occurred, baptism can hardly from the very beginning have been made to depend on prior circumcision.

Christianity, too, on proselytes and God-fearers was not inconsiderable. After 70, when Judaism ejected the liberal elements and became more rigid as regards the Law, the great company of God-fearers no longer found a home in the synagogue and the Hellenistic Jewish Christians shared the heritage of the synagogue with the Gentile Christians. This soon led in the West to the boundaries being eliminated between the two groups of churches which had originally been separated (see p. 65 n. 6).

In the East, on the contrary, Hellenistic Jewish Christianity presumably maintained its independent existence longer (see below), although it deserved and emphasized its description as *Jewish* Christianity less and less the more time passed and the further the churches were from Palestine.

The most significant influence of these churches on the early catholic Church consisted in the development and transmission of the synoptic tradition. This tradition is, of course, no unity. The material of the sayings source (Q) forms an independent group of traditions beside the narrative material, which Mark has handed down to us and which Matthew and Luke supplement by their matter peculiar to them; in addition there is the narrative of the passion and the resurrection which was handed down originally without the preceding material from the 'life of Jesus'.[39]

The account of Jesus' sufferings, death and resurrection was already developed in embyro, as I Cor. 15.1–5 shows, in Paul's time in the primitive Jewish-Christian church; it formed already in early days the basic confession of the Christian churches of Palestine. The narrative matter was added to it later in an expanded tradition fed from a variety of sources; Paul and two generations of writers in the Church after him did not as yet pay any attention of this material;[40] it appeared or was accepted essentially in Hellenistic Jewish-Christian circles. Q contains very old traditions; yet these traditions did not have their early setting in the life of those churches whose 'pillars' and first spokesmen were James, Peter and John; their substance is derived to a large extent from traditions about Jesus before the days of the Church; I look for its earliest setting in the life of these churches to which references

[39] Cf. R. Bultmann, *History*, pp. 275ff.; M. Dibelius, *From Tradition to Gospel*, ET 1934, pp. 178ff.
[40] Cf. W. Schmithals, 'Paulus und der historische Jesus', *ZNW* 53, 1962, pp. 145ff.

were made on p. 34 n. 71 para. 2; the literary sources used by Matthew and Luke contained this early matter, yet it was already stamped with a churchly impress which we owe to the same circles in which the synoptic tradition as whole was at home, namely the Hellenistic Jewish Christianity of the Eastern church. The fact that the synoptic tradition ranked as 'apocryphal' right up to Justin[41] points as clearly as possible to the relative independence in which the Hellenistic churches of Jewish-Christian origin lived in the East of the Roman Empire—also in Asia Minor—as late as into the second century.[42]

These brief concluding remarks lead back to the beginning of our investigation. The formation of the New Testament canon is determined by the combination of two circles of tradition, separated up till then, so that the Pauline writings and the synoptic tradition become the *common* subject-matter of the Church's confession. Thereby—presumably without any of the actors in this significant process being aware of it—an enterprise was brought to an enduring conclusion. The foundation of this enterprise was laid by the fathers of the two traditions by means of the memorable agreement in Jerusalem. The fellowship uniting Paul and James, in which there was a peaceable agreement to differ, was no other than the fellowship which unites the synoptic with the Pauline parts of the New Testament Canon.[43] Whilst in Jerusalem the emphasis on 'to differ' could not be avoided, now 'peaceable' has remained the sole determining factor. Whether rightly so is a question which neither the partners of the Apostolic Council nor the (Roman?[44]) circles responsible for the formation of the Canon can absolve us from answering. To find the answer remains the permanent task of all endeavours to frame a theology of the New Testament.

[41] Cf. *ibid.*, pp. 156ff.
[42] Cf. besides pp. 61f. and p. 65 n. 6 above for the group of problems touched upon here; they deal with the churches of Paul and Peter existing side by side, i.e. the Hellenistic churches of Gentile-Christian and those of Jewish-Christian origin. In addition and above all I refer to my book *Apostelamt*, pp. 244–55, where the attempt was made to prove that the twofold concept of apostleship which we find in the New Testament goes back to this double strain in Hellenistic Christianity.
[43] When matters are regarded in this way, does F. C. Baur now come into his own after all? Perhaps; but if so, then with a meaning very different from what he intended.
[44] *Apostelamt*, pp. 255ff.

BIBLIOGRAPHY

Bold type indicates the short titles by which works are cited.

ALTHAUS, P., AND OTHERS, **Die kleineren Briefe** *des Apostel Paulus* (NTD 8[7]), 1955
APPEL, H., *Einleitung in das Neue Testament*, 1922
ARNDT, W. F., AND GINGRICH, F. W., *A Greek-English Lexicon of the New Testament* (ET of Bauer's *Wörterbuch*), 1957
BARRETT, C. K., 'Paul and the "Pillar" Apostles' in *Studia Paulina: in honorem J. de Zwaan*, ed. J. N. Sevenster and W. C. van Unnik, 1953, pp. 1ff.
BARTH, F., *Einleitung in das Neue Testament*[3], 1914
BARTH, G., 'Matthew's Understanding of the Law', *Tradition and Interpretation in Matthew*, ET 1963, pp. 58–164
BAUER, W., **Rechtgläubigkeit** *und Ketzerei im ältesten Christentum*, 1934
'Jesus der Galiläer' in *Festschrift für A. Jülicher*, 1927, pp. 16–34
BAUERNFEIND, O., *Die Apostelgeschichte* (THKNT V), 1939
BEYER, H. W., *Die Apostelgeschichte* (NTD 5[4]), 1947
Billerbeck, P., and Strack, H. L., *Kommentar zum Neuen Testament aus Talmud und Midrasch*, 1922ff.
BORNKAMM, G., *Die Vorgeschichte des sogenannten zweiten Korintherbriefes* (Sitzungsberichte der Akademie zu Heidelberg, 1961, 2)
—— 'End-expectation and Church in **Matthew**', *Tradition and Interpretation in Matthew*, ET 1963, pp. 15–51
—— 'Der Philipperbrief als paulinische Briefsammlung' in *Neotestamentica et Patristica*) Freundesgabe Oscar Cullmann (Novum Testament Suppl. 6), 1962, pp. 192ff.
BOUSSET, W., in *Die Schriften des Neuen Testaments* II: *Die Briefe*[2], 1908
BULTMANN, R., *Exegetische Probleme des zweiten Korintherbriefes*, Uppsala, 1947
—— **Theology** *of the New Testament* I–II, ET 1952–5
—— **History** *of the Synoptic Tradition*, ET, 1963
—— 'Zur Auslegung von Gal. 2.15–18' in *Ecclesia semper Reformanda*: Theologische Aufsätze E. Wolf zum 50. Geburtstag, 1952, pp. 41ff.
CADBURY, H. J., 'The Hellenists' in F. J. Foakes Jackson and K. Lake, *The Beginnings of Christianity* I 5, 1933
CONZELMANN, H., *Der Brief an die Kolosser* (NTD 8[9]), 1962
CULLMANN, O., **Peter**: *Disciple—Apostle—Martyr*, ET, rev. ed., 1962
DALBERT, P., *Die Theologie der hellenistisch-jüdischen* **Missionsliteratur** *unter Ausschluss von Philo und Josephus*, 1954

Bibliography

DANIÉLOU, J., *Théologie du Judéo-christianisme*, 1958
DIBELIUS, M., *An die Thessalonicher I, II; An die Philipper* (HNT 11²), 1937
—— *Studies in the* **Acts of the Apostles**, ET 1956
DIX, G., *Jew and Greek*, 1953
DOBSCHÜTZ, E. VON, *Die Thessalonicherbriefe* (Meyer X⁷), 1909
FÉRET, H. M., *Pierre et Paul à Antioche et à Jérusalem*, 1955
FOERSTER, W., 'Die δοκοῦντες in Gal. 2', *ZNW* 36, 1937, pp. 286ff.
—— 'Stephanus und die Urgemeinde' in *Dienst unter dem Wort* (Festgabe für H. Schreiner), 1953, pp. 9–30
—— *Neutestamentliche Zeitgeschichte* I², 1955; II, 1956
FRIDRICHSEN, A., *The Apostle and his Message*, Uppsala, 1947
FRIEDRICH, G., *Der Brief an die Philipper* (NTD 8⁹), 1962
FUCHS, E., 'Hermeneutik?' *Theologia Viatorum* 7, 1960, pp. 44ff.
GEYSER, A. S., 'Paul, the Apostolic Decree and the Liberals in Corinth' in *Studia Paulina*: in honorem J. de Zwaan, 1953, pp. 124ff.
GOPPELT, L., *Christentum und Judentum im ersten und zweiten Jahrhundert*, 1954
GOGUEL, M., *La naissance du christianisme*, 1955
—— *Les premiers temps de l'église*, 1959
GRASS, H., **Ostergeschehen** *und Osterberichte*², 1962
GRUNDMANN, W., 'Das Problem des hellenistischen Christentums innerhalb der Jerusalemer Urgemeinde', *ZNW* 38, 1939
Haenchen, E., *Die Apostelgeschichte* (Meyer III¹⁰. 1956/III¹³, 1961)
HAHN, F., **Mission** *in the New Testament*, ET (SBT 47), 1965
HARNACK, A. VON, *Die Briefsammlung des Apostels Paulus*, 1926
—— *Marcion*², 1924 (reprinted 1960)
HAUPT, E., *Der Brief an die Philipper* (Meyer IX⁷), 1902
—— *Zum Verständnis des* **Apostolats** *im Neuen Testament*, 1896
HOFMANN, K. VON, *Der erste und zweite Brief Pauli an die Thessalonicher*², 1869
HOLTZMANN, H. J., *Die Apostelgeschichte* (Handkommentar zum Neuen Testament I, 2³), 1901
HOLTZMANN, O., *Das Neue Testament* I, II, 1926
HUMMEL, R., *Die Auseinandersetzung zwischen* **Kirche und Judentum** *im Matthäusevangelium*, 1963.
JONAS, H., *Gnosis und spätantiker Geist* I (FRLANT 51)², 1954; II, i (FRLANT 63), 1954
JÜLICHER, A., *Einleitung in das Neue Testament*⁵,⁶, 1906
KÄSEMANN, E., 'Die Legitimität des Apostels', *ZNW* 41, 1942, pp. 33ff.
—— *Das wandernde Gottesvolk* (FRLANT 55)², 1957
KLEIN, G., '**Besprechung** von E. Haenchen, *Die Apostelgeschichte*', *ZKG* 68, 1957, pp. 362ff.

Bibliography

KLEIN, G., *Die zwölf Apostel* (FRLANT 77), 1961
—— 'Gal. 2.6-9 und die Geschichte der Jerusalemer Urgemeinde', *ZTK* 57, 1960, pp. 275ff.
—— 'Die **Verleugnung** des Petrus', *ZTK* 58, 1961, pp. 285-328
KÜMMEL, W. G., 'Das literarische und geschichtliche Problem des ersten Thessalonicherbriefes' in *Neotestamentica et Patristica*, 1962, pp. 213ff.
LEIPOLDT, J., *Die urchristliche* **Taufe** *im Lichte der Religionsgeschichte*, 1928
LIECHTENHAN, R., 'Paulus als Judenmissionar', *Judaica* 2, 1946, pp. 56ff.
LIETZMANN, H., *An die Korinther* (HNT 9^4), with supplement by W. G. Kümmel, 1949
—— *An die Römer* (HNT 8^4), 1933
—— *An die Galater* (HNT 10^3), 1932
LIGHTFOOT, J. B., *Saint Paul's Epistle to the* **Galatians**[10], 1896
LIPSIUS, R. A., *Die Briefe an die* **Galater**, *Römer, Philipper* (Hand-Commentar zum Neuen Testament II, 2^2), 1892
LOHMEYER, E., *Die Briefe an die Philipper, Kolosser und an Philemon* (Meyer IX^9), 1953
LUEKEN, W., in *Die Schriften des Neuen Testaments II: Die Briefe*[2], 1908
LÜTGERT, W., *Gesetz und Geist*, 1919
—— *Die Vollkommenen im Philipperbrief und die Enthusiasten in Thessalonich*, 1909
MEYER, E., **Ursprung** *und Anfänge des Christentums* III, 1923
MICHEL, O., *Der Brief an die Römer* (Meyer IV^{10}), 1955
MUNCK, J., **Paul** *and the Salvation of Mankind* (ET of *Paulus und die Heilsgeschichte*), 1959
PREUSCHEN, E., *Die Apostelgeschichte* (HNT 4), 1912
REICKE, B., *Diakonie, Festfreude und Zelos*, Uppsala, 1951
—— **Glaube und Leben** *der Urgemeinde*, 1957
REITZENSTEIN, R., *Die hellenistischen Mysterienreligionen*[3], 1927
SCHLATTER, A., *Die korinthische Theologie*, 1914
—— *Erläuterungen zum NT* II^4, 1928
SCHLIER, H., *Der Brief an die* **Galater** (Meyer VII^{10}), 1949
—— *Der Brief an die Epheser*[2], 1958
SCHMIEDEL, P. W., *Die Briefe an die Thessalonicher und an die Korinther* (Hand-Commentar zum Neuen Testament II, 1^2), 1893
SCHMITHALS, W., *Das kirchliche* **Apostelamt** (FRLANT 79), 1961
—— *Die Gnosis in Korinth* (FRLANT 66), 1956
—— *Paulus und die Gnostiker* (Theologische Forschung 35), 1965
—— 'Die Häretiker in Galatien', *ZNW* 47, 1956, pp. 25-67
—— 'Die Irrlehrer des Philipperbriefes', *ZTK* 54, 1957, pp. 297-341
—— 'Die Irrlehrer von Röm. 16.17-20', *Studia Theologica* 13, 1959, pp. 51-69

Bibliography

SCHMITHALS, W., 'Zur Abfassung und ältesten Sammlung der paulinischen Hauptbriefe', *ZNW* 51, 1960, pp. 225–45
SCHOEPS, H. J., *Paulus*, 1959
—— **Theologie** *und Geschichte des Judenchristentums*, 1949
—— **Urgemeinde,** *Judenchristentum, Gnosis*, 1956
—— *Aus frühchristlicher Zeit*, 1950
SCHUBERT, P., *Form and Function of the Pauline Thanksgivings*, 1939
SCHÜRMANN, H., 'Wer daher eines dieser geringsten Gebote auflöst . . .', *BZ* 4, 1960, pp. 238ff.
SCHWEITZER, A., *The* **Mysticism** *of Paul the Apostle*, ET 1931
SIEFFERT, F., *Der Brief an die* **Galater** (Meyer VII⁹), 1899
SIMON, M., *St* **Stephen** *and the Hellenists*, 1958
STRECKER, G., *Das* **Judenchristentum** *in den Pseudoclementinen*, 1958
—— *Der Weg der* **Gerechtigkeit** (FRLANT 82), 1962
—— **'Christentum** und Judentum in den ersten beiden Jahrhunderten', *EvTH* 16, 1956, pp. 458ff.
TÖDT, H. E., *The Son of Man in the Synoptic Tradition*, ET 1965
TRILLING, W., *Das wahre Israel*, 1959, esp. pp. 138–59
WEGENAST, K., *Das Verständnis der Tradition bei Paulus und in den Deuteropaulinen* (WMANT 8), 1962
WEISS, J., *Über die Absicht und den literarischen Charakter der* **Apostelgeschichte**, 1897
WENDT, H. H., *Die Apostelgeschichte* (Meyer III⁹), 1913
WETTER, G. P., 'Das älteste hellenistische Christentum nach der Apostelgeschichte', *ARW* 21, 1922, pp. 397ff.
WILCKENS, U., *Die Missionsreden der Apostelgeschichte*, 1961
ZAHN, T., *Einleitung in das Neue Testament* I³, 1906; II³, 1907
—— *Der Brief des Paulus an die* **Galater**², 1907

INDEX OF AUTHORS

Althaus, P., 41, 42, 73, 75

Baltensweiler, B., 99
Bammel, E., 112, 113
Barrett, C. K., 41
Barth, G., 109, 110, 111
Bauer, W., 16, 27, 29, 37
Bauernfeind, O., 31, 94
Baur, F. C., 68, 88, 90, 105, 106, 117
Beyer, W., 87
Billerbeck, P., 22, 29, 64, 91, 94, 96, 97, 98, 100
Bornkamm, G., 86, 109, 110
Bousset, W., 98
Braude, W. G., 61
Braun, H., 103
Bruce, F. F., 19
Brun, Lyder, 98
Bultmann, R., 14, 17, 19, 21, 22, 28, 31, 73, 75, 90, 98

Cadbury, H. J., 16, 17, 26, 27, 29
Caird, G. B., 19
Chrysostom, 16
Conzelmann, H., 20, 58, 86, 90
Craig, C. T., 17
Cullmann, O., 27, 30, 45, 50, 51, 52, 62, 98, 103, 104

Dalbert, P., 21, 29, 61
Daniélou, J., 30
de Wette, W. M. L., 99
Dibelius, M., 18, 31, 34, 38, 57, 62, 85, 99, 116
Dinkler, E., 52, 101
Dix, G., 67, 72
Dupont, J., 63

Elliott-Binns, L. E., 33, 34
Eltester, W., 58
Eusebius, 51, 62, 99

Féret, H. M., 63
Fridrichsen, A., 46, 47, 57
Friedrich, G., 21
Foerster, W., 18, 45, 55, 60, 90

Geoltrain, P., 30
Geyser, A. S., 98, 107
Grass, H., 59
Grundmann, W., 17, 26, 29, 31, 37, 56
Gutbrod, W., 16, 26

Haenchen, E., 16, 17, 18, 19, 20, 23, 24, 28, 30, 31, 32, 38, 40, 42, 46, 49, 50, 52, 54, 57, 58, 59, 63, 71, 77, 81, 82, 83, 85, 86, 87, 91, 93, 96, 97, 98, 99
Hahn, F., 39, 98
Harnack, H. von, 22, 31, 61, 95
Hasler, V., 110
Haupt, H., 44, 45, 56, 57
Higgins, A. J. B., 31
Hirsch, E., 37, 62
Holl, K., 33, 79
Holtzmann, H. J., 32, 46, 50, 58, 60, 92, 99, 101, 102
Hopfner, T., 26
Hummel, R., 48

Irenaeus, 99

Jeremias, J., 31, 34, 87, 111
Josephus, 29, 67, 97
Justin, 99

Käsemann, E., 22, 111, 112
Kilpatrick, G. D., 72
Kittel, G., 49, 68, 114
Klein, G., 21, 23, 24, 25, 32, 49, 58, 66, 83, 84, 113
Klijn, A. F. J., 30

Index of Authors

Klostermann, E., 41
Knopf, R., 87
Köster, H., 106
Kuhn, K. G., 16, 60
Kümmel, W. G., 16, 28, 29, 34, 35, 52, 66, 97, 106, 109

Leipoldt, J., 61
Lerle, E., 61
Liechtenhan, R., 45, 56
Lietzmann, H., 17, 26, 48, 57, 62, 69, 75, 76, 80, 81, 97, 101
Lightfoot, J. B., 69
Lipsius, R. A., 39, 45, 47, 68, 72, 74, 81
Lohmeyer, E., 34
Lohse, E., 80
Loisy, A., 99

Manson, T. W., 31
Marxsen, W., 33, 35
Menoud, P. H., 25
Meyer, E., 38, 39, 46, 48, 60
Meyer, R., 22
Michaelis, W., 56
Minucius, Felix, 99
Michel, O., 81
Moule, C. F. D., 16
Munck, J., 37, 46, 56, 63, 67, 69, 76, 88, 90, 110, 114

Nock, A. D., 88
Norden, E., 86

Oepke, A., 76
Overbeck, F., 99

Peterson, E., 35
Philo, 29
Preuschen, E., 56, 71, 88, 90

Reicke, B., 17, 22, 39, 67, 73
Reitzenstein, R., 86
Rössler, D., 22
Rudolf, K., 99, 105

Schäfer, K. T., 100, 101
Schille, G., 85
Schlier, H., 40, 42, 45, 47, 57, 73, 74, 75, 76, 107
Schmithals, W., 30, 42, 62, 77, 79, 83, 102, 104, 113, 116, 117
Schnackenburg, R., 80
Schniewind, J., 109, 110
Schoeps, H. J., 16, 36, 61, 68, 97, 101, 103, 105, 106, 108, 114
Schrage, W., 17, 28
Schrenk, G., 34
Schrieber, J., 113
Schürmann, H., 110, 111
Schütz, R., 33
Schwartz, E., 31, 88
Schweitzer, A., 45, 64
Sieffert, F., 39, 40, 45, 46, 47, 69, 73, 74
Simon, M., 16, 17, 19, 21, 27
Soden, H. von, 107
Söden, R., 86
Stählin, G., 101
Strecker, G., 21, 26, 37, 48, 101, 106, 109, 110

Tertullian, 99
Thyen, H., 18, 21
Tödt, H. E., 112
Torrey, C. C., 33
Trilling, W., 110

Waitz, H., 97
Warner, D., 107
Wegenast, K., 67, 107
Weiss, B., 39
Weiss, J., 17, 35, 89
Wendt, H. H., 18, 31, 87
Wetter, G. P., 17, 27, 28, 31, 58
Windisch, H., 16, 27
Winter, P., 22

Zahn, T., 39, 45, 46, 47, 63, 66, 69, 72, 74

INDEX OF NEW TESTAMENT PASSAGES DISCUSSED

Matthew
5.17–20   109
8.5–10   111
10.5f., 23f.   111f.
17.24–27   109 n. 18

Mark
7.24–30   111

Acts
4.36f.   31 n. 64
6.1–8.3   16–37, 26f., 36
6.1–7   16–18
6.11   20
6.13f.   27
7.1–53   21 and n. 28
8.1   19
8.4f.   31
9.27   31 n. 64
9.29   27
9.31   33
11.19–30   30–36
11.20   17, 27, 31
13–14   52f.
13.1   31
15.5, 24   108

Acts
15.29   97–102
15.36–41   71
16.1–3   93–95
18.1–8   61
18.18   96
21.15–26   85–96
21.17   87f.
21.20   88f.
21.21   36 n. 79
21.25   97–102
21.28   27f., 36 n. 79

Romans
9.1–5   53
11.13f.   53, 57
15.19–21   52
15.30f.   79–84

I Corinthians
7.18–20   49
7.19   29 n. 56
9.5   51
9.20   56 f.
16.1–4   83 n. 12

Galatians
1.21f.   32
1.23f.   24
2.1–10   38, 50, 83f. n. 13
2.1   42
2.2   39–42
2.4f.   107
2.6   84 n. 13, 98
2.7f.   47, 49 n. 31, 51
2.9   45f., 49 n. 31
2.10   79–84
2.11–21   63–78
2.12   66f.
2.13   71f.
2.14   68f.
2.15–18   72–78
5.6   29 n. 56
5.11   25 n. 39, 37 n. 82
6.12   25 n. 39, 37 n. 82
6.15   29 n. 56

I Thessalonians
2.14   36 n. 77

125

www.ingramcontent.com/pod-product-compliance
Lightning Source LLC
Chambersburg PA
CBHW050839160426
43192CB00011B/2088